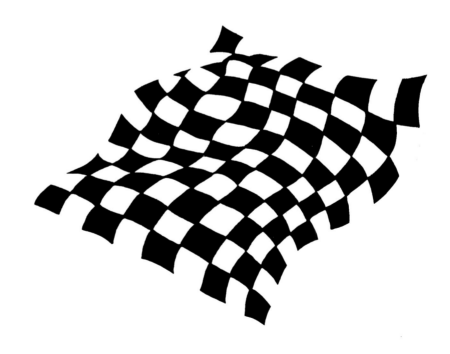

The Cruel Sport

Grand Prix Racing 1959—1967

Text, Photography, and Design by

Robert Daley

This edition published in 2005 by Motorbooks
International, an imprint of MBI Publishing
Company, Galtier Plaza, Suite 200,
380 Jackson Street, St. Paul, MN 55101-3885 USA

First published in 1963 by Prentice-Hall
International, Inc.

Motorbooks International titles are also available at
discounts in bulk quantity for industrial or sales-
promotional use. For details write to Special Sales
Manager at Motorbooks International Wholesalers
& Distributors, Galtier Plaza, Suite 200, 380 Jackson
Street, St. Paul, MN 55101-3885 USA

The photos are now part of
The Klementaski Collection, © 2005
PBM 219—65 High Ridge Road, Stamford, CT
06905-3814, USA www.Klemcoll.com

ISBN 0-7603-2100-0

Printed in China

Also by Robert Daley

Novels

Nonfiction

Pour P. avec tout

Contents

Prologue

New Canaan, CT
February 2005

THE FIRST GRAND PRIX I ever saw was at Monaco, May 1958. There were sixteen starters, of whom eight would die at the wheel, four of them before the year was out. Two more would crash, survive in a diminished state, and never race again.

That first year's body count shocked me—of course it did, who wouldn't be shocked—but I was new on the circuit, hadn't known any of the four very well, and so did not mourn in a personal way as I would later. Also, I thought that that season had been an aberration. But more drivers were killed the next year, and the next, and the next; this was out of never more than twenty men, and in as few as seven races a season, not sixteen or eighteen as now. Death in car racing began to seem to me not only inevitable, but almost normal.

During those following years I got to know the drivers well. They were young men like me, and they talked of getting killed all the time, which astonished and confused me.

There was very little television in Europe as yet. The cars were not rolling billboards as now, but were painted the national colors—red for Italy, yellow for Belgium, blue for France, green for Britain, silver for Germany, and so on—and had big numbers on their sides. They not only carried no advertising decals, but no video cameras or radios either. The circuits were public roads, and they were big: five miles around, eight, fourteen. Parts of them were so distant and so inaccessible to spectators that many, even most, of the crashes took place in private. Press and public learned of them second hand, beginning most likely with false or misleading information from the public address announcer: "So and so has had a shunt out on the circuit, nothing to worry about." We would lean forward watching the ambulances go out and come back in.

I WAS 27 years old at the start. I was trying to catch on with the *New York Times*, catch on with somebody, by working as a stringer. A stringer is someone not on the staff who has an "arrangement." Often he's a local reporter in an area where the paper has no resident correspondent. In my case, for most of the first three years, I was a stringer only. I paid my own expenses and cabled reports to New York for which I would be paid $50 each, if they were used. In America, Grand Prix motor racing was considered a fringe sport. The *Times* had no great interest in it.

I was an unpublished writer. I had two novels and many short stories already in a drawer. I was desperate to get published and working as a stringer was perhaps the way. It was the only one I could see. I had to take it.

My career as stringer had begun two years previously at the Winter Olympics at Cortina d'Ampezzo. No expenses and $50 for each piece used. Though young, I understood, I don't know how, that in order to get noticed I would have to go to some corner where I could stand out, someplace too far for anyone else to bother with. The Winter Olympics in 1956 were not big news either—who cared about winter sports in Europe?

My wife and our first child, Theresa, six months old, stayed with her family in Nice, while I took a train across the top of Italy, sitting up all night in a third class carriage worrying about money.

At Cortina I wrote fourteen articles in seventeen days, earning what to me was a fortune. The subject of one of them was Spain's only entrant in the Games, a bobsledder known as the Marquis de Portago.

Heir to one of the oldest titles in Spain, Portago had had only two or three practice runs before buying a pair of $1,000 sleds, recruiting some cousins from Madrid, and entering the games. Bobsledding was the most dangerous event. During one of his first descents he lost control at great speed, was slung out, and was lucky not to be killed. But now, only a few days later, he had the fourth fastest time.

I decided that if I wrote about him I might earn $50.

He was a year older than I was, I learned. Enormously rich. Spoke four languages. His principal occupation was racing driver, actually. He was under contract to Ferrari. Those icy cold mornings in the snow he gave outrageously quotable answers to every question I put to him. How had he met his American wife? "One does not meet an American girl, she meets you." And what did she think of him racing bobsleds and cars? "I do not ask her, I am Spanish."

Portago was tall, with black curly hair worn very long, and almost black eyes. He was unshaven, chain smoked, and was dressed all in black. He looked like a pirate, or like one of his famous ancestors, Núñez Cabeza de Vaca, a sixteenth-century conquistador whose name and title he still bore. He exuded energy, charisma, sexuality—I didn't know what it was or how to describe it, but it was there. He said he would win the racing drivers' world championship before he was thirty, then retire.

Standing nearby was Gurner Nelson, who seemed to be Portago's major domo. I interviewed Gurner too. He said he doubted his employer would live to be thirty, because every time he came in from a race the front of his car was wrinkled where he had been nudging opponents out of his way at 130 miles an hour.

People were going to notice this piece about Portago, I told myself as I cabled it to the paper. They would see my name on top of it and maybe, just maybe, it would jumpstart my career.

It didn't. Not immediately, anyway.

I went back to New York. Motor racing had never interested me before, but now I began to watch the sports pages for race reports and to search out Portago's name, for I felt that I had discovered him.

He drove factory Ferraris in races at the Nürburgring, Le Mans, and elsewhere in Europe, and when the cold weather set in and the fast car circus moved to Buenos Aires, Nassau, and Havana, he raced them there too. Always Ferraris. Grand prix cars and sports cars both—as yet I did not know there was a difference.

There existed at this time a number of men's magazines. They specialized in adventure, not girls. America was not yet ready for bare breasts, which in many states would have got everybody arrested. I was not brave enough to approach such august publications, but there was also a second tier, including a magazine called *Cavalier*. I phoned the editor, met with him, showed my clipping on Portago, and suggested I write a full-length profile.

Portago would be racing in Florida in the Twelve Hours of Sebring in a few days time, I added. I could go there and interview him.

The editor nodded, and said he would get back to me.

He phoned that afternoon. By all means try the Portago profile, he said. Go to Sebring. If he bought the piece he would pay $400. If not he would pay nothing. Of course, the expenses were on me.

I FLEW TO TAMPA in the middle of the night when rates were cheapest, landing about four a.m., and waited for a bus across the waist of Florida to Sebring.

I found Portago's hotel, and he agreed to come downstairs and talk to me. We sat in the lobby. I was so inexperienced that I did not really know what to ask him. "Every curve has a theoretical speed limit," he said. "Let's say a certain curve can be taken at a hundred miles an hour. A great driver like Fangio will take that curve at ninety-nine point nine every single time."

Fangio was the reigning world champion.

"I'm not as good as Fangio," Portago continued. "I'll take that curve one time at 97, another time at 98, and a third time at maybe 101." He smiled. "If I take it at 101 I go off the road."

Later I would learn that he went off the road rather a lot.

Out at the circuit I found that the race had drawn not only the most famous drivers and race cars in the world, but also, if I can use the word loosely, some of the most famous magazine writers as well, all of whom were preparing profiles on, and were clustered around, Portago. There were men from *LIFE*, *True*, *Esquire*, *Sports Illustrated*. And me from *Cavalier*.

Partly this interest was due to the sports car craze then sweeping America. A part of the American market was tired of the usual Detroit behemoths that waddled around corners, tired also of Indianapolis racing based on brute speed and bravery. Indy racing had no chic at all. Chevrolet and Ford had recently come out with sports cars, the Corvette and the new two-passenger Thunderbird. Imported MGs and Triumphs were selling briskly, and the luxury car market had been invaded by passenger Ferraris which cost as much as $15,000 apiece, an outrageously high price. Road circuits had sprung up from California to Connecticut.

As if to feed this sports car craze there had now appeared, for the first time in America, the glamorous Portago, who was rich, cultured, sophisticated, bearer of a noble title, and handsome in a smoldering, Spanish kind of way. He was also a very fast driver. That he had not yet won a major race did not seem to matter.

In those years big time motor racing was a murderous sport, as I would soon enough learn. The excessive danger weeded out the timid, and all the drivers were brave, though none quite as brave, if that is the word, as Portago. According to certain of his rivals, he wasn't skilled at all, only fearless. He liked to pass in corners where, logically speaking, passing was impossible, they said. He would take dangerous corners at speeds they called foolhardy, if not plain stupid.

Some of them prophesied that they would soon be attending his funeral, perhaps before the present season was out.

There was an extravagance to Portago, a physical magnetism. It was in the way he held his body and used it, in the way his mouth moved, his head. There was a feeling of danger about him. He had big white teeth and a dazzling smile. He had only to climb into a race car to draw all eyes. Girls and women flocked around him. According to the gossip columns, there were two other women in Portago's life, in addition to his wife, and they were as celebrated as he. One was Dorian Leigh, the top model of the day, who had borne him a child (he had two with his wife), and the other was the beautiful Linda Christian, a minor actress who had once been married to a major actor named Tyrone Power. Portago's wife, no less a beauty than the other two, had been with him in Cortina, and I had interviewed her, but I did not see her that weekend. Perhaps now they were estranged.

At ten the next morning the race began, sixty-five cars and 143 drivers lapping a circuit that was a bit more than five miles around, and for the next twelve hours the booming noise never stopped. In some previous life the terrain had been scalped. It was totally bald. Not a house, not a tree anywhere. In many places its curves were delineated only by painted lines, straw bales, or rubber pylons. A few temporary bleachers rose up here and there, otherwise nothing. Sebring was not only the least dangerous place where these men raced, it was also by far the least interesting—though not to me. For twelve hours I was enthralled.

By what exactly I do not know. By the speed and danger, obviously. By the beauty of the cars. By the spectacle of men trying to master these sleek, deadly machines. Machines they had created but could not fully control.

By this new, extravagant world, about which I wanted to know more.

The noise was stupendous. It gave me a headache. I was enthralled anyway. At about seven p.m. the headlights came on, and three hours later under the lights the race ended. The winning car had lapped that stupid circuit 197 times. Portago's car, which had had no brakes since noon, finished seventh.

I went up and talked to him.

"I drove nine of the twelve hours," he told me. "My co-driver, Musso, was sick. Castellotti's death upset him, I think." Castellotti, another of Ferrari's contract drivers, had been killed a month before, and Musso would be killed the following year.

I did not say goodbye to Portago, for by then he was surrounded by journalists much bigger and more important than I.

I WENT HOME and began to write my article. So did they, I assume. I don't know how long theirs took to write. Mine took more than six weeks, for I saw almost as soon as I started that I had not asked nearly enough questions, had not acquired nearly enough details. I began to make phone calls, to run down obscure references to Portago. An article under Portago's own byline appeared in *Sports Illustrated*. In it he joked that the life expectancy of drivers on his level was about the same as that of Kremlin bigwigs, who at the time were being regularly stood up and shot. I had a job as publicity man for the Football Giants, and I worked on the article nights and weekends and even, with not much to do during those slow off-season days, at the office.

It seemed to me that my entire career rode on this one article for *Cavalier*.

Finally I turned it in. For the editor's reaction I did not have to wait long.

"The Twelve Hours of Sebring" had been run on March 23. Portago had no races scheduled until the Mille Miglia on May 12, to be followed a week later by the Grand Prix de Monaco and then the entire European season.

Point-to-point open road racing was the way the sport had begun, the first race being from Paris to Rouen in 1894, ninety miles, won at the breathtaking average speed of eleven miles per hour. The men rode high up, aiming the car at first with a tiller, only later with steering wheels as huge as ships' helms. In turns, or when bounding out of potholes, the cars were virtually uncontrollable, and once they got into or near the towns, they had to be pointed through tens of thousands of spectators pinched so narrow that a bicycle could scarcely have got through.

There were many of these open road races, more every year, most of them starting from Paris, the capital of cars: Paris-Berlin, Paris-Vienna, Paris-Madrid. Many of them resulted in carnage.

And in 1927 Italy started the Mille Miglia, the greatest of them all—the most difficult, the most dangerous, a thousand-mile sports car race over open roads. Each year it drew hundreds of entrants, millions of fans. The race plunged through villages, through major cities, it twice crossed the country's tortured central spine. All the major factories entered cars, and so did scores of individuals, some of whom were skilled, others of whom frightened everybody.

Portago did not want to enter that year, but Enzo Ferrari assigned him a car, informed him he was driving, and that was that. He wrote a letter to Dorian Leigh in which he commented: "My early death may well come next Sunday."

Think of the route as a huge broken rectangle standing on end. The start was at the northern city of Brescia. From there the road headed east, plunging south at Padua and angling toward the Adriatic coast, where it ran behind the beaches for more than 200 miles before turning west and crossing the mountains to Rome. There it turned north to Florence, climbing the Futa and Raticosa passes, and crossing the Apennines a second time, then coming down into Bologna where it flattened out, stretching flat and fast the rest of the way back to Brescia again.

The race began just before midnight. There were over 350 cars entered, the smaller ones going off first, starting at intervals. These cars and their amateur drivers were going to be strung out all the way to Rome. Portago's turn did not come until 5:31 in the morning.

The ordinary roads of Italy on a Sunday in May. Lampposts, bollards, curbs that could tear off a wheel, houses, fences, walls, embankments, alleys of spectators, a stray dog perhaps, or some amateur enthusiast's car sideways in a blind turn—there was plenty to hit.

Portago was not alone. In the passenger seat rode Gurner Nelson, the major domo. In the tradition of the old open road races many drivers carried passengers that day, pals usually, navigators sometimes, company of course, and perhaps useful as muscle if the car slid into a ditch. Nelson had been an elevator operator in one of the hotels frequented by Portago and his mother, and had latched on to the boy. Though older, he had become a friend, if not quite an equal.

The Ferrari team had fuel and tire depots at Ravenna, Pescara. At Rome where Portago again took on fuel he was told he lay fifth. Linda Christian, his current girlfriend, was there. Dirty and sweaty as he was, he pulled her down and kissed her. This kiss lasted long enough for a photographer to run up and snap a memorable photo that would be published around the world. But many people, though they saw the romance in this kiss, were puzzled, for it wasted so much time.

There was another depot at Florence—he was still fifth—and the final one at Bologna, by which time he was fourth. A little later he was third and gaining. Could he have won the race?

Beyond Bologna he had the pedal floored. He rocketed through Goito, and was making top speed, about 170 miles per hour, as the faded walls of Guidizzollo came into sight. He had come more than 960 miles. The finish line was now about 30 miles ahead, the road so straight and flat he could almost see it. The car could go no faster than this. In less than ten minutes he would be there.

SOME YEARS LATER I went to Guidizzollo and stood on the verge at the kilometer 21 milestone.

The roadside ditch, I saw looking down, was just a ditch. Storied and all that, but unremarkable. Did I expect more? I had never seen it before today. Much was written about it at the time, always by people who never saw it either. None of us, the so-called world press, was here when the catastrophe—in more ways than one—occurred. Victims and perpetrator only.

Today, the ditch looked shallower than the old photos made it appear. Well, it was deep enough. It functioned like one of those slots on a roulette wheel as the croupier calls out "no more bets," and the slot catches the little ball. It brought this part of the world to a stop, the bets were collected, and the game was over.

The village wasn't—isn't—big. A huddle of tile roofs, the houses under them dating back, some of them, two or three hundred years. The victims came out this far to feel the sun, have a grand view. Above the ditch is a low embankment, which was where most of them were sitting or standing. The sun had started down. They were high enough to see what was coming, as if, in the strict sense, one can ever see what's coming.

In a fraction of a second a good many things and people came to an end. Though I was 4,000 miles away, something ended for me too, or so I learned the next day, so that afterwards I would never again look at life in quite the same way.

According to witnesses the car inexplicably swerved left and shot off the road. I have seen a number of explanations. A blown tire was one. A cracked half axle, damaged when the car slid into a curb many miles back, was another. Portago, it was said, knew about the half axle, knew also that the tire was rubbing on the frame or fender of the car, making an eventual blowout inevitable, but chose to bet he could make the finish line first. Was he that daring, that mindless? I am satisfied no one really knows what he knew or what exactly went wrong.

According to witnesses the car's tail walloped this embankment here, uprooting milestone 21—this milestone—before guillotining that telephone pole, or a predecessor, and leaping into the air. The pole as it fell snapped its wires, which flailed wildly, and then collapsed. All this in an instant. I am trying to slow the accident down. It happened so fast that the details the witnesses gave may or may not be accurate.

The car evidently careered across the road and up that embankment over there, where it scythed down two boys. It was in the air now, and it sailed back to this side where it slaughtered seven or eight more, all of whom were standing. Others, who were seated on the embankment were missed completely; the car went right over them. Finally it dropped low enough to be snagged by the drainage ditch I was peering into earlier.

Ten or eleven spectators had been killed; I have seen both figures. The Mille Miglia had been killed too. As an open road race it was never run again.

Portago and Nelson had been flung out. There were no seatbelts in race cars in those days. When a car collided with something its driver or drivers went flying. The machine itself disintegrated as well, and men and spare parts danced on the air all mixed up. Nelson was found in one piece. Portago was found twice. That is, the hood of the car had lashed back and cut him in two.

IN NEW YORK I heard the news on the radio in midafternoon. I was listening to hear who had won the race. In my head I had been living with Portago night and day for weeks, and the shock and grief I felt were as personal as if he had been my brother. So young, only a few months older than I, so full of life. Alive one second, dead the next. How could this be? These are cosmic questions that everyone gets to consider sooner or later, but I was asking them for the first time, and I lay awake most of the night mourning this man I had hardly known, and trying with tortured reasoning to find answers.

I had not immediately considered how his death might affect my profile of him, but the next day my phone rang at work and a secretary at *Cavalier* said she was mailing the manuscript back. To what address, she asked, did I want it sent?

The American magazine industry was not much interested in dead men, it seemed. The big name writers who had hounded Portago at Sebring had fared no better than I. *LIFE* eventually published only three or four pictures, with brief captions, under the headline: "Death Finally Takes a Man Who Courted It."

The pieces submitted to *Esquire* and *True* were rejected outright, and never mind the prestige of the men who had written them. But I didn't realize this, and I doubt that knowing it would have helped me much. My magazine career seemed over before it had even started, and I did not know what to do next.

BUT AFTER some weeks I got out my list of second tier magazines. The next name down was *Coronet*, an imitation *Reader's Digest*. The editor was named. A day or two later I forced myself to dial him. I said I was a freelance writer with some story ideas that might interest him. He said to come on over, so I did.

I did have some ideas—culled from the daily newspapers—but they failed to hold his attention. So I showed him my Portago clipping from the Winter Olympics. I doubted I had any real hope of interesting him in this subject. Rather I was making a somewhat desperate attempt to impress him with the only credentials I had: See, I am a published writer, look at this six-hundred-word article in the *New York Times*.

But immediately he looked alert. His magazine might be interested in a story on the dead Spanish Marquis, he said. "Call it 'Death of a Nobleman'—how does that sound?" If I wanted to try writing such an article, that's what my slant should be, he said.

No expenses of course, no guarantee.

I went home and worked another six weeks. "Alfonso de Portago was in love with life," I wrote, and for 3,000 words I mourned him. I quoted another driver, Jean Behra. "Only those who do not move do not die," said Behra who, incidentally, was about to be killed himself. "But are they not already dead?" I tried to write a straightforward article, but it filled up with grief. Grief for this dazzling young man dead so young. Grief probably for myself as well. Today I see clearly enough that Portago was a fool rushing toward violent destruction with a grin on his face and a cigarette dangling from the corner of his mouth. Not a meteor whose flame, after a minute, flamed out. He was, and had always been, a car crash waiting to happen.

But that wasn't the way I saw him then. A year or two ago when one of the glossy car magazines asked permission to reprint this article I reread it still again. Though not something I am particularly proud of, I took their money and let them do it.

When my manuscript was finally finished I carried it over to *Coronet*. Several weeks passed during which I heard nothing. Finally I screwed up enough nerve to phone the editor. He didn't think the article good enough, he told me as gently as he could, but he had passed it on to the other editors. We would wait to see what they had to say.

I was on the road with the Giants when a letter finally came from *Coronet*. The verve and feeling with which I had written about Portago, the editor wrote, had overcome his original misgivings. They were buying the article for $500. And congratulations.

FEELING a bit more confident, I went back to Europe the following year. I had one or two second-tier magazine assignments, but my principal connection was still the *New York Times*, I was still a stringer, and I started out on the Grand Prix circuit for the first time. If I was to write interesting copy, I saw, I would have to get to know the drivers of course, and the circuits as well. I was feeling my way.

Nearly all European races were run on public roads or streets, sometimes streets with tram tracks in them. These circuits framed the cars and drivers, and the speed and noise, and this frame was lined with fences, ditches, curbs, lampposts, trees, houses. In my *Times* pieces I began to describe all this, sometimes poetically, or at least as poetically as I could manage.

The circuits were easy to learn, and also to love. The drivers were harder.

Peter Collins was 27. He agreed to an interview but not graciously. A somewhat surly young man, it seemed to me. He and his young American wife lived on his boat in Monaco harbor. I was living in nearby Nice, so I went to look at this boat one night. It was smaller than a trailer and moved up and down as the water did. But the idea of it sounded romantic to me, and probably to him as well. Collins always wore a brown fiberboard helmet. There were no space helmets then, no seatbelts, and no fireproof coveralls. The drivers wore street clothes, sat loosely in big roomy cockpits, and nobody wore a helmet any more serious than the one Collins did. On the day in Germany that his Ferrari went into the forest, catapulting him into the air, he was wearing a blue polo shirt. Witnesses described the red car mowing down real estate, and the "blue blur" overhead that sailed headfirst into a tree.

Luigi Musso, also a Ferrari driver, spoke no English and only a few words of French. I never said much more to him than "Bonjour." Estranged from his wife,

he traveled with his longtime girlfriend, and they seemed devoted to each other. Since there was no divorce in Italy at that time, this was the best relationship that would ever be available to them, unless the wife died.

Musso went off into a wheat field in France. The car climbed the embankment and at one point, according to witnesses, was three stories in the air with Musso floating above it. The kinetic energy stored up in race cars at speed is quite astounding. Musso's legal wife locked and blocked all the dead man's possessions. The girlfriend went back to Italy to ask Enzo Ferrari if there was not something, an insurance policy, anything. Ferrari knew vulnerability when he saw it, and kept her for many years.

Stuart Lewis-Evans was a little guy, no bigger than a jockey and only an also-ran, so I never got around to talking to him. He crashed in Morocco in the final race of the season. The car caught fire and he did not get out of it.

The world champion that year was the Ferrari driver Mike Hawthorn, a tall, blond young man who always wore a bow tie when racing. Always. He considered this important. It was his style. Being new to the sport I didn't know this, and asked him about it. Apparently I phrased the question badly. "How come you're wearing a bow tie today?" I said.

"You don't notice much, do you?" he answered curtly, and walked away.

Reporters frequently get snubbed, especially by athletes who don't think that anyone contributes to their fame and fortune but themselves. Politicians and entertainers, who know better, snub reporters much less often. Asking questions entails certain risks to one's ego, and a reporter had best get used to it. Hawthorn, driving a Jaguar, a saloon car as the British call them, was killed racing a friend on a public road near London. It was just past noon. He clipped an oncoming truck, then skidded into a tree.

That was that year. There were two more the next, six gone already. Harry Schell, who was killed testing a car in the rain at Silverstone, was always described as an American living in Paris—he ran a bar there, or someone ran it for him. I interviewed him at a back table. We talked of Portago for a time. They had been great friends, had once shared a car at the 1,000 kilometers of Buenos Aires. Portago had picked this famous race for his debut in motor racing, but he didn't yet know how to shift gears. Schell had had to show him. American or not, Harry Schell spoke English with a strong French accent. He was one of the oldest drivers, 39. He told me that Grand Prix racing was not dangerous at all if you knew your limit, and stayed within it, as he did, and I carefully noted this down.

You almost couldn't tell, but Jean Behra had a plastic ear, the original having been rubbed off his head in a crash. He was a Ferrari contract driver but got into an argument with the team manager and slapped the manager's face. Enzo Ferrari fired him.

The German Grand Prix was held on the pre-war Avus track in Berlin that year. Behra was driving his own Porsche in a preliminary race when killed. One end of the track was banked. The car entered the banking on the proper line, but immediately began climbing. The animal was trying to get out of its cage. Higher and higher it climbed. In a moment it had wrested control from its driver. A second or so later it threw him out altogether. The top of the banking was lined with flagpoles, one of which Behra hit about halfway up. It broke him almost in two. I didn't see this. I went rushing around interviewing people who did and then sent still another grim report to the *New York Times*.

Already I was acquiring a certain reputation in the small and insular motor racing world, and not one to my liking. It must be understood that the enthusiast magazines—they are legion in all the countries—concentrate on camshafts and gearboxes. Fatal accidents are scarcely mentioned, never dwelt on. One sentence is usually enough. On lap three, or lap ten, so-and-so had a shunt that proved fatal. Shunt is a British word. No one ever hits a tree or wall at great speed, they have shunts.

I was writing something else entirely, and in a journal with weight, and certain of my colleagues were distressed. I was hurting motor racing, they felt, and behind my back I was sometimes referred to by some of them—the journalists, not the drivers—as Death Daley.

The drivers' attitude was quite different. Often they talked about getting killed. The nearness of death was what made them special, they felt.

The Berlin papers carried a photo of Behra in his open coffin, plastic ear in place, face serene. Beside the coffin stands Count Von Trips, his hand on the dead man's cheek. A photographer must have led Trips, who had won the race, to the funeral home and posed him.

This picture chilled me. I'm not superstitious, never have been, never expect to be, but felt as chilled as if I had seen a future I was not supposed to see. That there was death all around me, I knew very well. That these young men got much too close to it was obvious as well. Some of them would get out smiling. Perhaps not many, but some. Others would die, one of whom, the photo in some way made clear to me, would be Wolfgang Von Trips. It was as if I saw that photo as his death warrant.

He was not quite the next to go, but almost. Two rookie drivers, replacements for those who had been killed already, were killed during the Grand Prix of Belgium the following season. Then it was Trips' turn. When he went he took fourteen spectators with him.

FOR SEVEN SEASONS I went everywhere the fast cars went: to the Nürburgring, Zandvoort, Monza, Spa-Francorchamps, to Lisbon and Oporto, to Reims, Rouen and Le Mans, to Goodwood, Silverstone and Aintree, to Watkins Glen.

Among the magazine assignments I was able to get at this time was one from *Esquire* for a profile of the reclusive Enzo Ferrari, whose cars had won more races since the war than any other marque, and killed more drivers too, and I went to Modena hoping to interview him. Since I had no appointment I was apprehensive.

Phil Hill, who would soon be Ferrari's No. 1 driver as those ahead of him got killed, was testing cars at the Autodromo as I arrived. I watched this, and when he had finished he drove me around the track as fast as my Dauphine would go, not slowing down for the corners, sliding them all. The windows were open. I held onto the seat with both hands. Once he looked over and laughed: "That kind of thing doesn't even tickle my tummy anymore," he said.

At the hotel I asked him who I should call to get in to see Enzo Ferrari. He said he didn't know, and disappeared for a time. "He'll see you at three o'clock tomorrow," he said when he came back.

THE INTERVIEW took place in Ferrari's office at his factory. On a sideboard beside his desk stood six black-framed photos of his last six dead drivers, one of them Portago, and I kept glancing at them as he answered my questions. He had no English, at least none that he showed me, but spoke excellent French. He had no trouble phrasing exactly what he wanted to say, and much of it shocked me.

The legend was that he loved his drivers like sons, and never went to races because he could not bear to watch the risks they took. Was this true, I asked.

"A man builds something," he answered, "a beautiful machine. He puts all of himself into it. And then he goes to races and sees his machine, this part of himself, being maltreated, and—" He put his hand over his heart. "And so I do not go to races because it hurts me—here."

"You mean you suffer for the car, not the driver?"

"The driver too, of course."

Hill had stood silently in the corner. Afterwards he said bitterly: "I never thought he'd say something like that in front of one of his drivers. We all like to think he loves us because we are so brave and drive so fast. But deep down I guess we always knew he cares more about his cars than he does about us."

ALMOST THE last thing the *Times*' sports editor had said to me before I left New York was: "Get a camera. We pay fifteen dollars for every photo we publish." That sounded like big money to me, so I did get a camera, and the *Times* began to publish my photos which, in addition to the extra money, dressed up my stories. And then other publications bought photos from me too: *Esquire, Sports Illustrated,* the *Saturday Evening Post.* I had a cover on *Newsweek* once. In time the *Times* took me onto the staff and we moved from Nice to Paris. From then on expenses and allowances were paid; I was well paid. I continued to write my articles and columns. At the same time, as I became more and more enamored of photography, I bought better and better cameras until I had three Nikons and six lenses ranging from 28 mm to 300 mm. I used mostly Kodak Tri-X pushed to 800 ASA. I had no motor drive. Almost nobody else did either, for they were just coming into use. Day by day I took, I think, better and better pictures, all of them one of a kind, and I began to prepare a book about Grand Prix racing. It would be a big picture book and it would be beautiful, I hoped. To translate car racing into images that would have value would not be simple, because the three principal elements—speed, danger, and noise—cannot be photographed, or at least not easily. But I would try. I began to envision the book you are reading, my text, my design, 165 of my photos. And the title would be: *The Cruel Sport.*

Shortly after the book came out a driver named Bruce McLaren asked me to sign his copy. McLaren was from New Zealand, and he had a game leg from a schoolboy accident—he had fallen from a horse. A nice young man. Opening to the flyleaf I wrote: "When you are an old man I hope this book will help you remember how it was when you were young." Then I thought, as I handed the book back to him: but you won't live to be an old man.

And he didn't.

Part One:
The Men

1. THE GRAND PRIX driver works three hours a day some days. "Work" is to lie wrapped in his flimsy machine at speeds up to 160 miles per hour. He lies outstretched, his head forced forward by the 200 howling horsepower of his engine, and he slides around corners on the small of his back. The car weighs only 1,000 pounds; it is not much longer or thicker than the driver it encases. To save weight, the car is mostly aluminum, and its cowling is a thin sheath of fiber which, if it hits anything, will tear like cardboard. The driver will tear too. He, like the car, is fragile.

If, like Jim Clark of Lotus (opposite), the driver is under contract to a factory, he will race in nine or ten world championship Grand Prix each year, plus a number of other events, perhaps thirty in all. Although he receives a small retainer from the factory, most of his income comes from starting money paid by race organizers (about $2,000 per car for major races), and this is split 50-50 between him and the factory. Prize money, rarely more than $3,000 for first place, also is split 50-50.

Usually the driver practices Thursday, Friday, and Saturday and races Sunday, and for this he averages a bit over $1,000 a week for the weeks he works. The driver has much free time. If industrious, clever, or even just lucky, he can perhaps use it to double or triple racing income; he can endorse products, make appearances, or write learned articles for the technical press. But few drivers can manage this.

About twenty men in the world can really call themselves Grand Prix drivers, and this number includes perhaps fourteen who work for factories. The rest are independents, most of them in old or outclassed cars: young men on the way up, older men on the way down. For them there are fewer races to enter, much less starting money and usually no prize money at all.

For the favored fourteen, Grand Prix racing is a perilous life. But the money is good, the adulation grand, and they move in crowds and excitement all over the world.

2. THE GRAND PRIX driver is often a big man. Many, including Graham Hill, the 1962 world champion, are six feet tall or more. Big or small, they are very strong— strong in the hands and arms, in the legs, in the back, in the mind. A three-hour Grand Prix is a physical and mental wringing out such as few sports demand.

Basically, the driver is an athlete. He looks like an athlete, talks like one, thinks like one, and frequently trains like one. Many of the drivers were stars in other sports before turning to cars. Graham Hill was well known as an oarsman at Henley, Stirling Moss won many cups for equestrian

jumping, and the Marquis de Portago was the best gentleman steeplechase jockey in the world. Olivier Gendebien once ran 100 meters in 10.9 seconds; a professional soccer club begged him to sign a contract. Henry Taylor was the fastest driver on the British bobsled team long before he drove his first Grand Prix; "really, Grand Prix racing is the only sport," he said.

As athletes, very few were interested in team games. It was individual challenge which moved them. In the Army, Gendebien and Innes Ireland were paratroopers, and the late Harry Schell served in the Russo-Finnish War as a volunteer tail gunner.

5

3. GRAND PRIX DRIVERS differ from other athletes only in that they risk their lives. This brings to them a strong mystical streak, a feeling for the beauty of life and for the brevity of it, for the need not to waste what can only be enjoyed for a moment or two. This is not true of all, just of some. A few drivers are unaware of the world around them. Their interests are limited to spark plugs and gearbox ratios; nothing worries them and almost nothing frightens them.

Others love art, books, fine wines, music. Jo Bonnier (left) owns an art gallery in Lausanne. His private collection includes work by Picasso, Fernand Leger, and other modern masters. He has over sixty paintings in all; he hopes to build it into one of the world's great collections. Beauty is important to Bonnier; he says his wife is beautiful, as well as his son, and he remembers the 1959 BRM which he drove as "the most beautiful looking race car of all time."

Racing drivers are often collectors. Phil Hill collects classic old cars, classical records, and player piano rolls. Hill has over four thousand player piano rolls. He has two ornate old player pianos, both of which shine like new, and among the rolls is a Rachmaninoff etude played by Rachmaninoff himself.

4. OLIVIER GENDEBIEN dines often at fine restaurants like Maxim's in Paris. He loves to drink old wines with his meals and, with the coffee afterwards, to sip a *vieux marc de Champagne* from a crystal snifter. His home, in the forest near Fontainebleau, thirty miles from Paris, was once an old mill with a brook tumbling by it. Gendebien and his wife have done the mill over into a manor house, and dammed the brook to make a pool. It is a big stone house, centuries old, with ivy on the walls. There are lawns, big trees, rose bushes, and, leaning over the pool, smaller trees hung with moss. The brook splashes loudly through.

Inside, the house is furnished in antiques and works of art. There is an enormous old fireplace in the main room, with cups and trophies on the mantel, and the horns of a superb buffalo (shot in the Congo) hanging over that. The heavy wooden staircase and balustrade were hand hewn by craftsmen centuries ago, and the wood has been lovingly waxed and polished. Several eighteenth-century Flemish paintings hang on the walls. In Gendebien's study are more trophies and rows of leather-bound books. The Gendebiens believe in elegant living—and in children too: there are three very small ones about the house.

Racing drivers are often highly literate. Portago tried to read a book a day. Ireland's library includes books by Chekhov, Sophocles, Anatole France, Hugo, Conrad, Von Papen, Huxley, Kipling, and others.

5. THE GRAND PRIX driver may come from any part of the world: from Australia, like Jack Brabham (right), or from Argentina, Brazil, Mexico, South Africa, New Zealand, California, Texas, Sweden, Spain, Holland, Belgium, France, Germany, Portugal, and even Connecticut. But mostly in recent years they have come from Italy and Britain.

Their goal was and is the world championship, which is awarded on the basis of points scored in a handful of major races, between seven and ten in recent years. But very few have ever won it (only seven in thirteen seasons), and no one has ever won it in less than a very fast, very durable machine. Skill counts for much in motor racing. The car counts for more, and control of nerve counts most of all. The nerve of a race driver—to hold a machine on the line day after day at 150 miles per hour or more—is cold, calculated, and very difficult to sustain. For two years Brabham sustained it; he also had a very strong car and so he won the world championship twice.

Perhaps Brabham cannot sustain such nerve anymore; it is harder when you have money in the bank and a factory producing your own cars. But he was champion twice. He was the best.

It is impossible to know what the "average" driver does when he retires. Only a few ever do. Cliff Allison is farming, Tony Brooks runs a garage, and the great Fangio lives in wealth in Argentina. Many of the rest are dead. It is interesting that only Brabham, as this is written, ever cared enough about the machine itself to start his own factory, and to build and race his own car.

6. A DRIVER can be any age. Most are in their thirties, but Ricardo Rodriguez, propelled by his father, was a Ferrari team driver at nineteen. At twenty he lay in the wreckage of his machine. Men ran to him. "Don't let me die," he pleaded. "Please, don't let me die."

A nation wept for him. The President of Mexico walked in his funeral.

7. MAURICE TRINTIGNANT has been a race driver twenty-five years. He won the Grand Prix of Monaco twice, of Pau three times, but does not win much any more. He is forty-six and mayor of his town, Vergeze, where Perrier water comes from. There have been older drivers than Trintignant, but none younger than Rodriguez.

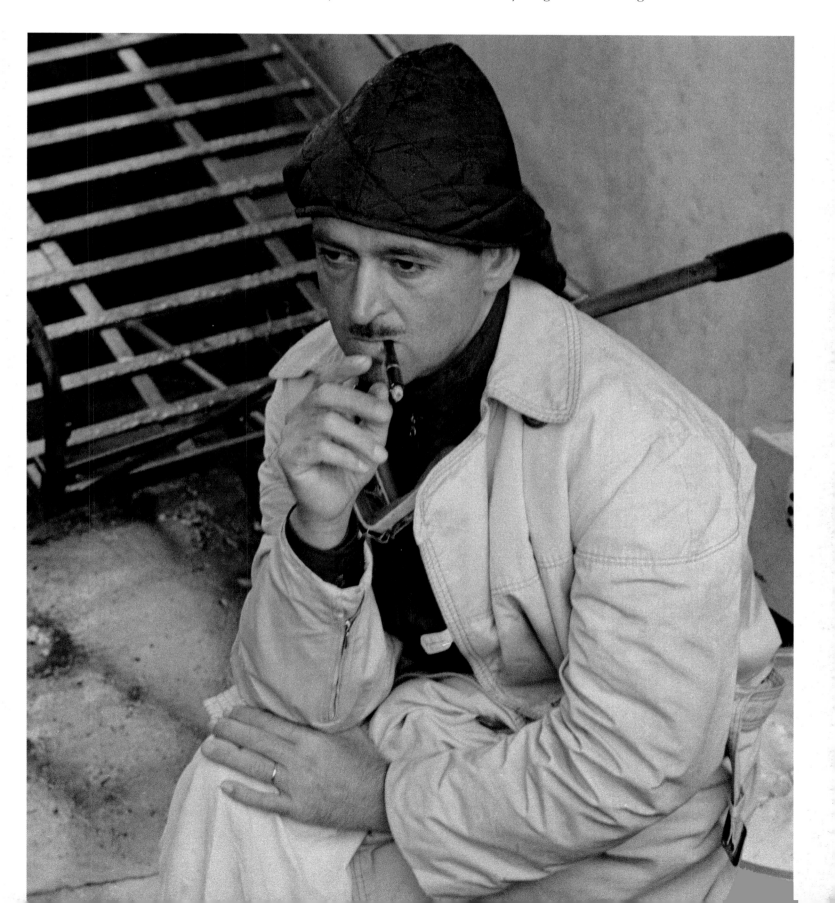

8. SOME DRIVERS come to car racing because, like Phil Hill, they love the way cars look. Others are led to the sport by their fathers, who not only pay all bills, but who signal frantically from the pits, urging Junior faster, faster. Sometimes the fathers were dentists like Papa Moss and Papa Brooks, or former train drivers grown wealthy through political favors like Papa Rodriguez. None ever seem to have the slightest notion that Junior is in any danger.

Bruce McLaren (left) fell from a horse when he was a schoolboy. He spent two years in a hospital, and one leg healed considerably shorter than the other. To help him forget, his father started him in car racing. The boy was good, the best there was in New Zealand. At nineteen, the New Zealand Grand Prix Association sent him to England for experience in faster cars. He caught on with Cooper, and was second in the world championship competition in 1960 at twenty-two. He is a polite, friendly, stocky young man, married, solid, steady. Perhaps the fast cars saved him from becoming an introvert, or worse.

9. WHEREVER HE comes from, the Grand Prix driver is a cosmopolitan young man. In recent years he has raced all over Europe, in the United States and Canada, in Australia and New Zealand, in South Africa, the Caribbean, and Mexico. He has shaken hands with Dictator Juan Perón of Argentina, with the King of Morocco, with the Queen of England. He has received his trophies from dukes and cabinet ministers beyond number; he has looked out from the cover of *Newsweek* or its equivalent in ten or more nations.

In Europe the sport is always called "motor racing" (never "car racing," or "auto racing"), and it is not really considered a sport at all. Most newspapers report it on the front page or on pages outside the sports section.

The Grand Prix driver not only has raced all over the world, he has been accepted in the best places all over the world too. He is believed to have what the world calls "class" and this is partly because he usually speaks one or more languages in addition to his own. Count Wolfgang von Trips (opposite page) spoke English, Italian, and French, in addition to German. He had taken the trouble to learn these languages perfectly—not only fluently, but without accent. This is very difficult to do. Portago, Schell, Bonnier, Gendebien, and, to a lesser extent, Moss and Phil Hill all know (or knew) three or more languages; many drivers know two.

At various times in the past, the language of racing has been German, Italian, and French, depending on who had the most drivers and the most cars. The language of racing is now English.

10. IN THE OLD DAYS most drivers came from a life of ease. Counts and Marquis and even a Prince or two lived and died on the circuits of Europe. There were always ex-mechanics, ex-motorcycle racers around (some of them the fastest drivers), but the dashing young noblemen dominated the sport, even when not winning. They gave it grace, verve, glamour, and a sense of tragedy.

Now the noblemen are gone, all of them. But many of the drivers still come out of luxury, like Giancarlo Baghetti (left), whose father is a Milan industrialist.

Baghetti was the first of the new wave of Italian drivers. Since Luigi Musso died at Reims in 1958, Italy had had no drivers at all. At first, mourning Musso, no one urged Italian youth toward the fast cars. But in 1961 a program was introduced and a Ferrari was promised to the fastest of the young Italians. Eventually, this car fell to Baghetti, then twenty-six. In it he won the first world championship Grand Prix he ever entered, at Reims later in the year, as if to quiet Musso's shade once and for all. The Ferraris were the fastest cars that day. They ran one, two, three, four for mile after mile. Then the three leading Ferraris broke down, and Giancarlo Baghetti, child of wealth, found himself leading the oldest, richest, most prestigious of all Grand Prix races. He might have panicked and lost, or panicked and crashed—so many cars harassed him so skillfully. Instead he won by inches at 119 miles per hour.

Most drivers go years before they win a world championship race, and some of the biggest names in the sport—Portago, Musso, Schell, Behra—never won any in their lives.

11.

THERE ARE NO noblemen now, and few enough rich young men. There are a great many ex-mechanics, and there is a single ex-motorcycle champion, John Surtees. Surtees was possibly the fastest motorcycle racer of all time. In 1956, then twenty-two, he won his first world championship, and he won six others before he quit to concentrate on cars in 1960.

Everyone said he was a natural, would be a great racing driver too. Surtees himself said nothing; he never says anything, except when he gets mad. In the 1961 Grand Prix of Italy, Bonnier swerved to avoid a flag marshal in the road. Surtees couldn't swerve. His car went up the back of Bonnier's car, over Bonnier's head, and left skid marks on Bonnier's front cowling on the way down. Both cars retired. No one was hurt. Surtees said to Bonnier, "I'll fix you for this. I'll fix you permanently."

Whatever is said in moments of panic such as this one, no driver would ever deliberately endanger another. Their lives are in each other's hands, and they know it. However, there are very few close friendships among the drivers. They often speak bitterly of each other. Partly this is because it is hard to forgive a man who has caused you to be that frightened, hard to be fond of him ever again.

Surtees is used to winning, but in cars he hasn't won much. He drives his machines into the ground trying. He is not known for gentleness or grace. He is a rough young man, always in a hurry.

12. A DRIVER can be coldly determined or, like Willy Mairesse, he can be nervous, impatient, slightly inaccurate. He can go off the road so often it begins to seem, to the others, only a question of time. Such men are called "crashers," and no one feels happy about their future. Such men appear to be insensitive to the exact play of the car, insensitive to their own lack of this sensitivity, and insensitive to the warning of others. There are always one or two like this each year.

13. OR, LIKE Harry Schell, a driver can love girls, laughs, and good living. Everyone liked Harry Schell. He was a prudent man. In eleven seasons he had never had an accident—nor won a major Grand Prix. He made plenty of money finishing fourth, third, second. "With me, racing is a business," he said. "I don't take chances." And he meant it.

If a driver has this philosophy, it might possibly save him.

It did not save Harry.

14. MOST DRIVERS are responsible professionals. Their job is driving race cars. They enjoy this job; they do it the best they can, and they think about it and talk about it all the time. Few drink. Few even smoke, and though there are always girls around the fast cars, most drivers are preoccupied, disinterested.

Richie Ginther even enjoys testing cars. Most drivers don't; they get no extra money and each test lap is still another chance to go on your head. But all drivers test, and all do it conscientiously.

All drivers go off the road from time to time, and every one has had at least one bad crash. They have no illusions; crashes are inevitable. Ginther crashed three straight times in 1962. A car he was testing in March caught fire, and he went to the hospital with burns. In May in Holland another car butted him off the road. In Monaco his throttle jammed open, he rammed several other cars, a wheel flew off and a spectator died. Ginther was soberer—and slower—for months.

If, in a crash situation, a driver reacts fast enough, he can usually walk away from it. This they believe. This is how they can go on. A few drivers seem to court accidents; the odds against crashers, the others feel, are one-hundred percent. But for the careful driver, the odds are not really steep.

15. THE DAY of the race is, for the driver, absolute concentration, intense nervous tension. It is terrible strain. It ages a man. When Dan Gurney was twenty-eight, new on the circuit, and about to start his third Grand Prix, he looked like this. His body was taut, his car fills his entire mind, but his face was smooth, unworried.

16. THREE YEARS, one victory, two crashes later, Gurney's face was lined, and sometimes before a race he could not manage the boyish grin very well. He had learned a lot, perhaps too much. His stomach churned all morning; he had found that taking tranquilizers sometimes helped, and sometimes didn't.

C.A.S. BROOKS.

28

17. RACING DRIVERS often race when badly banged up. They are expected to ignore broken ribs or arms, aching charley horses and the like, while being hurled about the cockpit for two hours or more at top speed. They are expected to concentrate on holding the pedal down, despite pain. They are not supposed to be scared, although if they hurt badly enough they cannot concentrate on what they are doing, and the driver who cannot concentrate is always scared.

At Le Mans in 1957, Tony Brooks missed a curve at three o'clock in the morning. The car ran up a sandbank, flipped over, and landed partly on Brooks, partly on the bank. Brooks couldn't move, and was worried about fire. Then a Porsche skidded around the same turn and knocked the car off him. Brooks found he had "tremendous cuts and abrasions. That pretty much took the go out of me for the rest of the season."

"If your ability isn't enough to win a race, don't try," said Brooks. "And if you ever frighten yourself, then you are going too quickly and you'd better slow down."

Because Grand Prix racing is so difficult, and so dangerous, only a handful of drivers each season are really trying. Some have lost confidence in the machine, or in themselves; some have begun to be troubled by thoughts of wife and children. Some are too old to put their lives on the line anymore; some know themselves too young and inexperienced to dare—yet. A few, through crashes, have become doom conscious.

In fourteen months, Tony Brooks won five Grand Prix races—a fantastic record. Then his marriage began to weigh on him; a daughter was born. He accepted a second-rate car for 1960; in it he would not have to try so hard. In 1961 he was slower still, and then he retired.

It was unusual that Brooks won five races, and unusual that he quit. But the elapsed time of his peak—two seasons—is about normal. Few men can sustain it any longer than that. When this peak has passed, most drivers race on—carefully. They keep banking the starting money. They have families to support and they worry that the starting money will stop.

18. THE SON of a veterinary surgeon, Innes Ireland trained as an engineer with Rolls Royce, first in Glasgow, later in London. Afterwards he served two years as a lieutenant in a Parachute Regiment in the King's Own Scottish Borderers in the Suez Canal Zone. Decommissioned, he ran a small engineering firm in Surrey. And began to race sports cars. Lotus was running outclassed, front-engined cars at this time, but in 1960 the first rear-engined Lotus appeared and Ireland was the driver who showed the world that Designer Colin Chapman was on to something—Ireland won three quick races and finished fourth in world championship points.

He had also got married. Nearly all Grand Prix drivers are married. Some have as many as four children. Most wives travel from race to race where they sit on the pit counters amid tools, tires, mechanics, and engineers. Some wives are bored, some work stopwatches and keep lap charts, and one or two are near frantic with worry every moment their husband is on the track.

It does not make much difference how the wives react; the drivers scarcely know they are there. Absorbed in his machine, the driver has room for nothing else.

More than that, the driver loves his job—despite its strain, despite its danger.

"My wife tolerates racing," says Innes Ireland. "She does not ask me to give it up. She knows I wouldn't."

Phil Hill:

FOR TWO AND a half hours the Grand Prix driver is cooked by heat, dulled by fumes. The wind tears at him, the noise batters his brain. His body is subjected to frightful pounding, and his mind, if he has one, usually has been pounded numb too. Hour after hour the trees rush by, the road slides sideways under his wheels. The car fights to get away from him, as if it has a life of its own.

At the end of the race, the driver's clothes are soaked through, his face is slack, his eyes unfocused. He is close to exhaustion. This is Phil Hill, second by 1.3 seconds in the 1962 Monaco Grand Prix, as he climbed from his car.

Race driving is a métier for hard, sure men. A driver cannot be stupid and survive, but introspection will ruin him just as fast. The Grand Prix driver must be hard physically and hard mentally, unable to imagine what will happen if he hits a tree at 160 miles per hour.

If he is to win often, the driver must have no thought except to beat down other drivers, to demoralize them with conversation off the course and tactics on it, to smash them.

Most—not all—of the top drivers are like this. But Phil Hill is a thoughtful, gentle man. "I'm in the wrong business," he said once. "I don't want to beat anybody, I don't want to be the big hero. I'm a peace-loving man, basically."

In sports cars Hill won the 24 Hours of Le Mans three times, the Sebring Twelve Hours three times, the 1,000 Kilometers of Buenos Aires, of the Nürburgring, and of Venezuela. In Grand Prix cars he was world champion in 1961; in seven races he was first twice, second twice, and third twice. He won the two fastest races of the season, the Belgian Grand Prix at 128 miles per hour, and the Italian Grand Prix at 130. He did not make a mistake all year.

Behind him are many track records, notably at the Nürburgring. There are 175 curves per fourteen-mile lap of the Nürburgring. They are curves of all sizes, shapes, and speeds, some at the bottom of long, steep downhill runs, some just after humpbacked bridges which send the car aloft, wheels dangling, reaching stiff-legged for renewed contact with the road. Worse, the road is narrow and alternately bordered by forests, by stone walls, by precipices and impenetrable hedges. If a car leaves the road, its driver almost certainly will be badly hurt, perhaps killed.

For thirty-five years it was said that no man would ever lap the Nürburgring under nine minutes. The great Fangio had not come close; his best was only 9:13. But in practice in 1961, in a car powered by an engine forty percent smaller than Fangio's, Hill lapped in 8:55, and in the race itself, with the course littered by slower machines, in 8:57.8.

HILL WILL TELL you he is not a brave man, but the evidence is to the contrary. He won his first Le Mans in 1958 by stomping on the gas instead of the brake in the middle of the night in a blinding rainstorm. More prudent drivers slowed, and when the storm eased, Hill was too far ahead to be caught.

He won once at Sebring in another blinding rainstorm.

"When you passed me, I was horrified," said the Swedish driver Jo Bonnier after the race. "You were laughing. I didn't see how you could stay on the road at such speed. What were you laughing about?"

"It amused me the way the rain was running down your beard," Hill replied. "You looked so uncomfortable."

At times like this Hill sounds as racing drivers are supposed to sound: aggressive, insensitive to peril. So he does when he says he is not very friendly with other drivers: "How can you be friends with a racing driver? You try to beat them all day on the

circuit, and then at night you're supposed to forget all that? I think all racing drivers secretly hate each other anyway."

BUT THEN the hard veneer disappears and he adds morosely: "Racing brings out the worst in me. I don't know what would have become of me if I hadn't become a race driver, as a person, I mean, but I'm not sure I like the person I am now. Racing makes me selfish, irritable, defensive. There are thirty other guys trying to get where I am. I have to be on my guard all the time. I even have to hang around the cars when I could be doing something useful, in order to make sure the mechanics are doing what I have asked them to do. We're not allowed to touch the cars. I don't hang around the cars all the time because I like to, but to protect my interests. If I could get out of this sport with any ego left, I would."

Hill pauses, then observes: "Life is a struggle whatever work you do, but at least in any other business you don't have to risk your life."

It is clear that the strain of the permanent danger weighs more heavily on Hill than on most other drivers. Drivers are always talking about death, often outrageously, as when Stirling Moss remarks: "Racing is a kind of Russian roulette. You never know when the chamber will come up loaded." The listener is always shocked, perhaps awed, and Moss basks contentedly in this reaction. Many drivers enjoy the danger, or say they do. Not Hill.

As he struggled to win the world championship, Hill was handicapped precisely because he did think of it, and because (as he says) his ego no longer needed the glory it once had sought. Certain risks he accepted. Others he would not accept.

In May of that year he dueled lap after lap with Jim Clark's Lotus, the two cars at great speed never more than a few feet apart. "There was a very fine ethical line which both of us recognized," Hill remarked afterwards. "Certain tactics were okay. Others were too dangerous. Some drivers would not have recognized this ethical line. There is one driver, for instance, who has a reputation for imprudence and who now uses this reputation as a weapon to scare other drivers

out of his way. I think that's evil." The implication is that Hill would refuse a dice with a driver he could not depend on, as he refused to dice with Trips in the British Grand Prix that same year.

Hill had gone directly from the French Grand Prix to Aintree, England, where he spent days walking, driving, studying the course. Suddenly a telegram arrived from Enzo Ferrari.

Ferrari wanted to know why Hill had not returned to the factory to test cars. Ferrari threatened to send no car for Hill for the British Grand Prix.

Ferrari harries his drivers, undermines them, perhaps feeling that a shaken driver will race faster than a confident one.

Now Hill worried until race day. Would his car come? He was shaken, all right, but into driving slower, not faster.

"Ferrari pressured Peter Collins like this just before Peter was killed," Hill muttered when he saw his car unloaded at last. "Now the same thing is happening to me."

The race began, Hill was still upset, and then rain poured down. On a tight turn in the rain Trips nipped in front of Hill. Neither driver had much traction, neither could see. Hill started after Trips, but was unsettled, had no confidence in himself nor in his machine in the blinding rain. Abruptly he dropped back.

"I'm not going to kill myself just to be world champion," he mumbled to himself.

He finished second to Trips that day.

PHYSICALLY, Hill is an almost perfect racing machine: keen eyes, strong hands, heavily muscled arms and shoulders. He has never had a serious accident in fourteen seasons of racing. He has rarely even slid off the road, and he cannot remember the last time he overstressed an engine.

But mentally Hill is different from most other drivers, for he is basically a gentle man in a profession devoid of gentleness. Motor racing is noise, speed, danger, crowds, constant travel, living often in seedy hotels out of suitcases jammed with dirty clothes. Many of the people in it tend to be callous, if not cruel at times.

Hill cannot seem to be cruel to anyone. Hordes of hangers-on, many of them rich, follow the races from country to country, buttonholing Hill and other drivers incessantly, begging for conversation, a ride out to the circuit, a cup of coffee on the terrace perhaps. "Where do these people come from, what are they doing here?" cries Hill. He resents them because "they make me see the phony side of all this," but he is polite to them nonetheless.

Interviewers plague him, often with stupid questions, but if he is driven to show annoyance, he will usually apologize contritely a few moments later. People attach themselves to him and he worries for days about how to get rid of them without hurting them.

Race day is an ordeal for him. "It is always the same," he says. "I'm asleep in a warm bed, the sun is shining in the window, and I start to wake up and I'm lying there all warm and secure. And then I start to think: this is not just any day. This is race day. Then in an instant all the warmth and security is gone, the bed is cold, and I sit up wide awake."

Hill genuinely dislikes the limelight, keeps no scrapbooks, sometimes refuses to read articles about himself, and, instead of displaying all the dozens of trophies he has won, he stores most of them in barrels in his cellar. When he wins a race he seems embarrassed as the flowers and trophies are heaped upon him; he tends to hang back in the crowd of officials and also-rans who are also part of the ceremony, and he will strike none of the triumphant poses the photographers beg him for.

There is gentleness also in the way he speaks of the danger he has faced for so many years: "I would so love to get out of this unbent. I have a horror of cripples. Even when I was a little boy I couldn't bear to look at anyone who was deformed, could not bear to see them suffering. I guess I've always worried about ending up that way myself. I want to get out of this in one piece. Do you know, I've never been hurt in an accident."

Ask him why he races and he will reply: "Because I do it well." What he means is that this is the only thing he does that well, meaning brilliantly. How can a man not do something which he knows how to do brilliantly?

No other driver I know of doubts the worth of racing. Most adore its glamour and excitement, and do not ask further questions. But Hill wonders all the time about the "intrinsic value of what I do. Does it have any intrinsic value? I have become a cynic. I no longer believe that driving race cars is so important." He would like to believe he contributes to the world, but his case is complicated by the risk he runs. If he crashed tomorrow, what exactly would he be dying for? The $20,000 or so he earns each year? Hardly.

PHIL HILL STANDS out as a vulnerable human being in a trade where nearly everyone else pretends to be invulnerable. Most others are surrounded by the mob and love it. At times, Hill also seems to enjoy the pressure and excitement, but mostly it just makes him nervous.

Periodically during the season he will sneak away between races and drop out of sight for days at a time. He never tells anyone where he has gone. He has many acquaintances, but very few friends and no intimates, male or female. When not preoccupied by a race, he is a very warm person. He invites close friendship, but when it is offered to him he backs off. No one can get close to him.

He loves music. He buys tickets to the opera outdoors in August in the Roman arena at Verona or to hear Joan Sutherland at La Scala in Milan. He invites the Gendebiens or the Ginthers to drive up with him, and they enjoy the performances, but not as much as he.

Between races he lies in his hotel room at Modena listening to symphonic music on a hi-fi rig which he has brought in and put together by himself.

Sometimes he says he hates racing.

What he really likes to do, and what he seems much better suited for temperamentally, is to restore old cars. He has ten of them at home in California: Pierce Arrows, Packards, an Alfa Romeo, all thirty years old or more, all gleaming and new as if built only yesterday. Hill has rebuilt them all with his own hands, starting usually with rusted hulks and decayed interiors, many parts missing or ruined. He has worked on one car for months at a time, sanding away the rust of decades, finding or making missing parts, polishing old chrome till it shines again like silver, restitching interior leather, cleaning, painting, perfecting down to the last ashtray. When working on a car he can go weeks without seeing anyone, without eating a proper meal, or getting a full night's sleep. When he has finished, the car looks and runs like new, a little bit of the luxury and elegance of the past lives again, and Hill himself feels a satisfaction which few races have ever given him.

Certainly this is an art form, and temperamentally Hill seems more of an artist than a race driver. He is as alert to sounds as any musician and his eye is as keen for detail as any painter's. He is forever noticing details others don't notice: a certain color, a certain view, someone else's inconspicuous habit or attitude. Hill can put a little artistry, a little perfectionism into racing—to take a corner on precisely the same line lap after lap after lap at 128 miles per hour is not easy—but not too much. Because in racing the primary thing is not perfect technique but winning.

It is significant that Hill likes sports car racing better than Grand Prixs, endurance better than sprints. In a sports car race, if a man drives perfectly for twelve hours or twenty-four he will win—time will destroy his opposition for him. But in Grand Prix racing a man must harry his opposition from beginning to end and somehow, at the crucial moment, get past it. Grand Prix racing demands what in sports is called "killer instinct," and this Hill lacks. He is not mean enough. He understands too well that others would like to win, to be champion, just as much as he. This robs him of the ability to work up a consuming (if temporary) hatred for his rivals, without which a really superior performance is impossible.

WHEN HILL was much younger, and fighting for a place on a factory team, he was, by his own admission, aggressive and a fool. He drove frantically, and rivals gave way out of fear. The years dulled that aggressiveness, but sharpened his skills until he was, in 1961,

at the age of thirty-four, as fast as, or faster, than any driver except, possibly, Moss. He was certainly faster than Trips most times. But in some races Trips would nervously hound him, pressure him, until Hill became nervous himself and feared being forced, or forcing Trips, into some ghastly mistake. He would feel a kind of panic; not trusting Trips' judgment in a race car, he temporarily did not trust his own, either. The stakes were too high to take a chance, and so he would give way to Trips.

In the end, the ghastly mistake Hill feared indeed occurred. Trips plunged into the mob and killed fifteen people, himself included. Hill drove on very, very carefully, very, very fast, winning that race and the world championship at an average speed of 130 miles per hour.

He had driven that whole season like a single long sports car race—preferring to race too cautiously, rather than too fast. A bundle of nerves inside, he made no mistakes; his rivals did make them, and so he won the world championship.

But in the tumult and gloom of the Trips tragedy, it went unnoticed that Phil Hill was champion of the world. Worse, the sentimental preferred to believe that Hill had not won, poor Trips had merely lost. Phil knew this. There was no pleasure in his victory. He felt empty and a little bitter. He had won the prize, and it was worthless. He took his trophies and went away, hoping that some day the world championship would mean something to him. But so far it has not.

When he came back to race for Ferrari again the next year, he was a different man. Much of the spirit seemed to have gone out of him, and after the first few races he did not really seem to care about his job.

"I no longer have as much need to race, to win," he said in a sad, puzzled way. "I don't have as much hunger anymore. I am no longer willing to risk killing myself."

He had raced for Ferrari exclusively for nine years, but at the end of that long, slow season Ferrari and Hill parted.

His friends did not know whether to weep or applaud, and apparently Phil Hill didn't either.

Stirling Moss:

THE YEAR WAS, for Stirling Moss, a purgatory, or perhaps a hell. His smashed body healed slowly, and he counted the pain of that as nothing. But the pain of loss was another thing: a year gone out of his life, a year without race cars, without the absolute control of a machine at speed, a year without what he loved in life above all things.

He crashed April 23, 1962, Easter Monday, at Goodwood, England, at roughly 100 miles per hour. No one can explain how or why, although many saw the crash and have tried. Moss himself remembers nothing. He was far behind following a long pit stop. He was hurrying, because Stirling Moss always hurried, always drove to the limit, always felt he owed maximum effort to his public and himself. He did not become Stirling Moss by lifting his foot at such times as that. The Lotus, with Moss in it, left the road, plowed across a field, and impacted itself against an earthen embankment. The wreckage folded nearly in two, and it took thirty minutes to cut Moss out. Nearly every bone on the left side of his body was broken. He lapsed into a coma. At the hospital, doctors believed he would not live out the night.

He was unconscious or semiconscious for thirty-eight days. He lay with forty-odd stitches in his face, his cheekbone puffed up by interior supports, and partially paralyzed down the left side; when he came out of his deep dream at last, his speech was slurred and he could not properly focus his eyes.

From a previous crash he had recovered extremely fast through exercises and determination, and now as he got stronger he tried this again, against doctor's orders, pushing his broken leg against the end of the bed, trying to walk to the washstand and back. Once he got dizzy halfway across, fell to the floor, and nearly passed out. The nurses found him trying to laugh at his weakness.

His progress that second month was swifter than the doctors had expected, and Moss himself became cheerful and busy. He gave interviews. His secretaries came in and he dictated thank-you notes at a furious clip to every well-wisher who wrote in. He conducted his business, enjoyed friends who came to see him, and amused them in return. He said he expected to be entirely recovered within two months, and to be back in a racing car that summer.

He said: "I'll go out to one of the circuits near here alone. If I cannot get down to the lap record in a few laps, if I find that my reflexes are not what they were, then I must retire. I could not bear it if continuing meant being with the also-rans at the back of the race."

The hospital room was a bright place now. Obviously Moss felt he had lost nothing. Around the circuits, other drivers spoke of him with admiration, and took bets on how soon he would be back.

But July passed, and August, and then September. Moss was up and about. He could dance, make a speech. He was asked to flag off races here and there, and did so, and banked fees. He was still Moss, though thinner, more finely drawn than before. He wore dark glasses to hide his sunken left eye. But he did not race nor try to, and he was not as cheerful as he had been. When he shook his head sharply, it took a moment or two before his eyes would focus again.

He underwent two eye operations. A tear duct was cleaned out, and then the left eyeball was lifted in its socket a millimeter or two—enough, Moss hoped, to restore normal vision.

As the months passed one by one, Moss made no more pronouncements about coming back to the cars which had been his life, and the silence around him was the saddest thing of all.

I went to see him a year to the day after the crash. He was friendly and cheerful, and he seemed gentler than I had known him to be. The day before he had been in

Stuttgart, and in the museum there had sat down in a pre-war Mercedes race car. He described how close the wheel was to his chest, how enormous the machines were compared to, say, a Lotus.

"Do you know," he said, "it was the first time since my accident that I sat down in a race car."

A whole year during which he had not sat down in a race car anywhere. He who had always loved the way a car held him. The way it felt around him. He had not got into one. Did he hate the machine that much, or fear it, or did he just not trust himself to sit in a race car he might drive away in? I didn't know and I didn't ask him.

Eight days after my visit, again at Goodwood, alone, he lapped the circuit for forty-five minutes in a Lotus sports car. Rain poured down, the road was slippery under his wheels and he soon knew that his reactions were down. "I don't react quickly enough anymore," he said when he stepped from the car. His voice sounded bewildered and deeply sad. "I felt like a man who had all the answers written down in a book, but had lost the book." And then he announced his retirement.

HE WAS ONLY thirty-two years old but he had already been racing sixteen seasons, more than any of those around him. The two photos here are of Moss before and Moss five months after. A few of the boys and men he started with just after the war have retired. Most are dead. Few ever drove more than a hundred races in their sometimes short lives, nor won more than a dozen times. Moss had driven 466 races to date, won 194 of them and earned three times as much money in racing and allied activities (e.g., endorsements, appearances, books on the sport) as anyone else—his estimated income has been $140,000 a year.

In England he was, and remains, a celebrity only slightly less well known and admired than the Queen herself, and everything he does is news. When he won a race, headlines reported "Moss Wins Again." If he lost, the headlines invariably read: "Moss Breaks Down" or "Moss Crashes" or whatever, and you would read on in the story to find out who actually did win.

When he was not racing, the papers reported instead his frequently unsuccessful business ventures, his faltering marriage (he is recently divorced), his speeding tickets, lawsuits filed against him (everything from failure to pay for a radiator to "negligent killing" after a race accident—he wins nearly all suits), or which girl he took dancing last night.

IN ENGLAND, where motor racing is as socially acceptable as polo or yachting, Moss was its most dedicated, successful figure and, as he says, he need only to spit to find himself written up on page one of a newspaper with a circulation of five million or more.

It is possible that no man ever loved motor racing as much as Moss, nor paid so heavily for that love in terms of time put in, miles traveled, marriage broken, accidents survived, or physical suffering endured.

Probably he had fewer accidents, in proportion to miles raced, than other drivers; but he raced so much more often than they, that the accidents he did incur were choice—more shocking (because of his superior skill) and more spectacular (because of the relatively higher rate of speed at which he was moving).

If his colleagues had been asked to name the best driver active, it is probable that Moss would have got every vote. But though unquestionably the best and fastest driver of his time, Moss never won the world championship. He did win sixteen world championship Grand Prixs, and it is a measure of his extraordinary versatility that he won them in five different marque cars: Mercedes, Maserati, Vanwall, Cooper, and Lotus, two of which (Cooper and Lotus) were not even factory owned or factory tuned. Lately Moss had chosen to try to beat expertly tuned factory models driven by the best men the factories could hire—with his own or other privately owned cars. This is roughly equivalent to a pitcher trying to win a ball game with no one playing in the outfield. It simply cannot be done regularly—except by Moss—and even Moss couldn't win the world championship doing it.

No active driver can match Moss' sixteen victories. The Australian, Jack Brabham, twice world champion, has won seven, all in a factory owned and prepared Cooper. Some people around racing wonder if Brabham, a fine driver, would be any good in another car. There was no such doubt about Moss.

Moss ALSO WON more sports car races than anyone else, eleven of which counted towards the world championship, and again in a variety of cars: Aston Martin, Maserati, and Mercedes. A sports car is roughly equivalent to what you can buy in a showroom, and all sports car races are for endurance as much as speed. The longest, Le Mans, lasts twenty-four hours, the shortest nearly eight. Sports car racing demands an entirely different technique: sensitivity to what the car will stand, the ability to judge pace, and tremendous stamina. Most sports car races are co-driven by two or more men. But when Moss raced in one, he would usually try to win single-handedly, giving the co-driver only a rare, brief turn at the wheel. That way he got more racing, which he loved, and more applause, which he loved too. Moss in motor racing has been the equivalent of a musician able to play six or seven instruments—and who is a virtuoso in all of them.

Exclusivity, to Moss, was as much a prize as victory. If every man could be a racing driver, he said, he would have to find something else. He loved loneliness and glory, and the danger was fine with him because it weeded out thousands of men who might equal his skill but couldn't match his control of nerves.

"To race a car through a turn at maximum possible speed when there is a great lawn to all sides, is difficult," he said, "but to race a car at maximum speed through that same turn when there is a brick wall on one side and a precipice on the other—ah, that's an achievement!"

Moss IS THE SON of a dentist who had raced as a young man and had followed the sport for many years. Stirling was born September 17, 1929. As a child, he pleaded to be allowed to sit on Daddy's lap and steer the family car, and when he was about ten years old he begged for and received the present of a very old and dilapidated 7-horsepower Austin. The Moss family had a small farm at the time, and Stirling fashioned his own private circuit out of lanes and paths and spent months driving wildly about in clouds of dust as fast as the battered little car would go.

At eighteen, he got his first driver's license, and with it the right to race on public circuits. He sank all his savings into a tiny race car and began entering the hordes of local races which Britain, now that cars and gasoline were back at last following the war, had begun to stage. Stirling won eleven of the first fifteen races he entered and was on his way.

It was not just that the boy had found something at which he could excel. Motor racing at that time in that country was the thing to do—it made you one with all the best people. In 1950 over a hundred thousand people watched the British Grand Prix, including King George VI, the Queen, and Princess Margaret.

Moss was not the only young Englishman to succeed on the race circuits of the world during this period. There were many others. But Moss was first, won more often, confined himself almost always to British cars, and conducted his affairs so skillfully off the track that he was soon snowed under by fame and money.

If he loved to race, he loved money no less, and saw no reason why the two couldn't be combined. Soon he was racing all over the world, in South Africa, South America, Australia, New Zealand. Before Moss, racing had been a sport limited to six months of the year. Moss probably was the first to see it as a year-round business. Year after year he raced forty or more weekends, traveled 150,000 miles. He demanded and received top starting money, as much as $2,000 per race for himself (with a similar amount going to the owner of the car), and usually he could match this amount with prize money by winning the race itself—for who else in those early years could be bothered going so far away from Europe? Many of the drivers do now, but it was Moss who showed them how profitable this could be.

BEFORE HE WAS twenty-five, Moss had seen that the writing of books could set him apart from his fellows. He now has written six. The first, *Stirling Moss' Book of Motor Sport*, has sold over 100,000 copies in many different countries and languages. He has written all these books the same way, by speaking into a tape recorder. One took only three-and-a-half days to "write" and he has earned from them, relatively speaking, a phenomenal amount of money. He says that racing in strange lands boosts book sales there, and that the books, by increasing his fame, boost the amount of starting money he can command. He says books and racing complement each other very nicely.

Moss did not invent endorsements, but he brought to them more of himself than anyone else did, by selling not only himself but his services too. Let BP gasoline (one of his sponsors) announce a sales push, and Moss would start moving about the nation, gas station by gas station, sometimes using a helicopter so that he could crowd more and more appearances into a day.

At each stop he would talk to customers (and delighted owners, of course) about BP gasoline and about Stirling Moss. He is an extremely articulate man. Nearly every man (and many women) in the British Isles cares something about cars, and mobs of people would overflow the gas station for the chance to chat with Stirling Moss. Around motor racing, it was said that Moss collected £10,000 ($28,000) a year for lending his name to BP, a figure Moss neither confirmed nor denied.

Most drivers do nothing but drive. During the season they practice Thursdays, Fridays, and Saturdays, then race on Sundays. The other three days each week are mostly for loafing, and the entire off-season is for loafing or hobbies. Moss never loafed and never slept more than six hours per night. If he raced in Vienna on Sunday, he was back in his London office on Monday afternoon and usually worked until midnight or later.

He answers every letter he receives, 10,000 or more per year, employs two secretaries and a manager, and must make quick decisions on a multitude of business problems. He collects everything that is written about himself and carefully pastes clippings into scrapbooks that by now nearly fill a room. Racing reports go in one scrapbook, articles on what he calls his "personal life" go in another. The ratio of clips is four to one in favor of his personal life. This annoys him, but there is nothing he can do about it, and he is too wise in the ways of public relations to complain. Reporters who ask questions about his marriage receive answers which are as courteous (though not as complete) as those he reserves for questions on racing. He says that she was tired of living out of a suitcase, of traveling so much, of never having a home. He says that he had thought, when they married in 1957, that this wouldn't matter, but, "Obviously, it did matter. I can see that now." He does not blame their separation, which lasted from 1959 to their divorce in May, 1963, entirely on racing; he merely cites racing as a contributory factor.

THERE IS PROBABLY some vanity in his keeping all those scrapbooks, but it must be understood that Moss writes his books out of them, slowly flipping the pages while he talks into his recorder. His is probably the most completely documented life in sports. Everything he does gets into the papers.

When he lost his driver's license one year for dangerous driving, his trial was reported in full. He is a very fast driver on public roads (some of his colleagues refuse to ride with him out of fear), and he had been in trouble with the traffic department before. But now as his license was withdrawn for a year, all of Britain chuckled at a cartoon which one of the papers carried. The drawing showed a Caspar Milquetoast type in an old, old car chugging past a panting cyclist. The Milquetoast type is saying to his wife: "I don't like to brag, dear, but I think I've just overtaken Stirling Moss."

Moss is five feet seven inches tall, muscularly built, nearly bald. He is a serious man. He is always on time for appointments and expects others to be. He can speak creditably in French and Italian. A few years ago he was so serious as to seem humorless to some, but as he gets older he is becoming more and more relaxed and it is pleasant to talk to him. He laughs a lot now, often at himself. But he cannot speak lightly of driving race cars, which to him is an art form. It is the thing he did better than anything else in the world, better than anyone else in the world.

"I love to feel a racing car around me, the way it holds me. I love to make it do all that it was built to do, and then a little bit more—for instance to hold the throttle open ten feet further into the turn this time than the last time, and then ten feet more the next time than this time.

"A racing car is an animate object, not an inanimate one. It has character. There are things it will do and things it won't do. Your job is to find out what it will do and then push it as far as possible. But you mustn't push it too far or it will turn on you, as a person would.

"I love to race a motor car which has been properly designed and built. But if a car is unreliable, if a car is a bastard, that is not an agreeable thing at all. Even though you might be able to control it better than someone else might.

"I have no desire to build a car myself, only to take something someone else has built and extract the maximum from it. I guess you would say that I am a conductor rather than a composer. I would be no good as a jazz musician. I don't want to improvise, merely to play the music exactly as it is written. If I were a painter I wouldn't like to mix my own paints, merely to take paints already mixed and make the best possible picture out of them. I suppose that would make me a bad painter.

"It is a fine thing to win, to hear your country's anthem played just for you, but I believe I like the competition better than the victory, the fighting better than the winning. I like to feel the odds against me. That is one of the reasons why I do not drive for a factory. I want to beat the factory in a car that has no right to do so. If I had any sense I would have been driving for Ferrari all these years. But I want to fight against odds, and in a British car.

"Of course, racing is dangerous. I like it that way. Without danger there wouldn't be any point to it, really. It would be just a game that anyone could play. It would be like climbing a mountain with a net ready to catch you if you fell. What's the point to that? You might just as well walk up a ladder. Racing's a gamble. I like to gamble, to bet I can do something no one else can do."

LIKE ALL DRIVERS, the safe ones as well as the crazy ones, Moss has had plenty of crashes and broken nearly every bone in his body except his neck. His worst crash previous to Goodwood occurred June 18, 1960, at Spa, Belgium.

"I was holding the car in a sweeping right-hand bend at 140 miles an hour when the left rear wheel snapped off. I did the only thing possible under the circumstances. With the wheel gone the rear of the car slid out left, I threw the steering hard left to correct, and stood on the brakes. I reckon I took fifty miles per hour off the top. Yes, I must have done at least that. I remember looking back and seeing that the wheel wasn't there anymore. The car spun I think twice and hit the embankment backwards. I think my neck snapped back and knocked me out. I don't remember getting thrown out of the car or flying through the air. The next thing I remember is being on my hands and knees in the dirt. I think I landed that way, but am not sure. I wasn't scared in the car because I was too busy. But I was scared now on my hands and knees. I thought I was going to die. I couldn't breathe, you see. I couldn't see either, and that worried me, but mostly I couldn't breathe."

Another driver, Bruce McLaren, stopped and ran up. Moss asked McLaren for artificial respiration, which McLaren refused, not knowing what might be wrong with Moss. "Bruce was wise, there," says Moss today.

At the local hospital x-rays disclosed that both legs, his nose, some ribs and three vertebrae were broken. Moss hurt so much he had to have morphine. He was slapped into plaster. The doctor told him he'd be in plaster up to his neck for at least three months.

"I didn't like the sound of that," Moss says. "They were very nice to me there, but I told them I wanted to get back to England right away." Two days later he was flown home. He put himself in the hands of a specialist "whom I always go to for broken bones."

The doctor looked at the x-rays, removed all plaster, and said: "All right, let's see what you can do."

"I was afraid," says Moss, "that any brusque movement might snap my spinal cord. The doctor assured me that this was impossible, that I could do anything the pain of which I could stand."

This was all Moss needed to hear. Three days after the crash he was going up ropes hand over hand in the clinic's gym "in order to keep my arms and shoulders in shape." He would do leg and stomach exercises in his bed until he fell asleep from exhaustion, and when he woke up he would do some more.

Soon the days became routine: two hours in the gym each morning, two hours in the swimming pool each afternoon. His secretaries came in twice a day, for he had received thousands of letters of sympathy. "I answered them all. It was hard work, but I did it." Evenings a writer from a British film studio came by to talk to Moss about every aspect of his life, for a movie is to be made about him.

The exercising day after day was accompanied by pain, which Moss ignored. "It depends upon what you understand as pain. It was nothing I couldn't stand. It wasn't so bad."

After three weeks he was bicycling about the grounds. After four he used to duck out nights to go dancing. In the fifth week he tested a car at Silverstone and broke the lap record. No crowd watched him do this, but characteristically he calls this the biggest thrill of his incredibly swift recuperation.

SEVEN WEEKS after losing a wheel at 140 miles an hour, breaking both legs, some ribs, three vertebrae, and his nose, Stirling Moss won a race in Sweden. Two weeks after that he went to Portugal for the Grand Prix. Organizers rejected his entry. No man could be whole after such a crash, they said. Moss went to their offices. He jumped about. He performed deep knee bends. The puzzled Portuguese conferred, then agreed he could race. Moss left the building laughing.

Whenever he talked of this crash later, Moss seemed to feel a curious elation. From the instant the wheel flew off, until final recovery, moment by moment, day by day, he had had exactly the right reflex, done exactly the right thing. Telling the story he seemed to me proud, thrilled all over again. Deep inside, I think he exulted in being not only a faster driver than others, but more "man" too. He was stronger in mind, body, will, heart. He could do what he had to do. He had proven it, and he came to feel that man—that Stirling Moss at least—could do anything in the world, anything at all, if he wanted it badly enough. This was his creed. "I believe that if I wanted to run a mile in four minutes, I could do it," he said once. "I would have to give up everything else in life, but I could run a mile in four minutes.

"I believe that if a man wanted to walk on water, and was prepared to give up everything else in life, he could do it. He could walk on water. I am serious. I really, practically believe that."

His sword was steel. Stirling Moss could do anything.

But this time it is more than a few broken bones. On Easter Monday his brain was touched. Who knows where the human will is? Perhaps that was touched as well. This time Moss cannot change anyone's mind with deep knee bends, not even his own.

He has been hurt, and it has gone deep inside him, and so perhaps at last he is finished with the fast cars, finished with the flashing, thunderous machines he loved so much.

If so, what is to become of Stirling Moss? Oh, he has money enough put aside, and trophies, and scrapbooks—and memories of what it was like, the car tight around him, the world passing in a blur. Without that, what is left for Stirling Moss?

Life stretches ahead, vast and empty. He will get used to it in time. But what about right now? The world has known few bereavements such as his.

Graham Hill:

THERE ARE NO CLOWNS in car racing, no guitar players, no vaudeville performers. The drivers are mostly good humored. They find things to laugh about. But mostly their wit is dry and droll; you don't have to laugh if you don't want to. The funniest driver is Graham Hill—he is also one of the most serious.

He is a big man with a neat black mustache. The deadpan expression on his face never changes in a racing car, and rarely when he is making people laugh.

As a youth, Hill worked five years for S. Smith and Sons, clockmakers. Did this mean he was himself a clockmaker?

"A clockmaker," Hill explains thoughtfully, "is usually a little old man with white hair and thick spectacles, very studious and clever, if sometimes a bit cockeyed. I don't think I could have been called a clockmaker. Nice of you to ask, though."

Hill did his military service in the peacetime Navy, sailing about the Mediterranean on training maneuvers in the engine room of a cruiser.

"We were always being notified that we had been sunk," says Hill. "It was that type of ship."

He left the Navy certified as "capable of taking charge of a boiler room while steaming under full power," and in 1951, when he was twenty-two, learned to drive a car.

At twenty-three he saw an ad for a racing driver's school at Brands Hatch. He went down from London to see what it was like.

It cost five guineas (about $15) to join the school, and five shillings (about $.70) per lap after that. Hill loved driving the tiny (500 cc) old racing car, but didn't see how he could continue at those prices. So he hired himself out as unpaid mechanic to the fellow who had the school, and when this school folded, Hill joined another on the same terms—meaning lack of terms.

"On the basis of my vast experience," he observes, "I was soon promoted to school instructor." He sprinkled his conversation with esoteric terms ("oversteer, understeer, shunt—stuff like that") gleaned from racing magazines. His pupils were very impressed, he says.

BEING UNEMPLOYED, he drew thirty-two shillings a week on the dole, enough to pay bus fare to his non-paying job. After a few months he began to feel he was worth a salary, say £3 a week, $8.40. The owner of the school refused.

Graham did not want to quit, but how can you work for a man who says you're not worth $8.40 a week?

Being twenty-six and eager to get married, he joined Lotus as a mechanic and for two years begged for a chance to drive the race cars. For two years Colin Chapman, the owner, rejected him.

Again Hill felt honor bound to quit. Four months later, Chapman asked him back as driver. Hill raced Lotuses for the next three years in the Grand Prix series. The cars were terrible. Once Hill finished as high as sixth. Club Lotus was so pleased it voted him a trophy for "the outstanding performance of the year by a Lotus driver."

"I couldn't stand much more of that," Graham recalls.

He quit Lotus for BRM, in whose cars he was to win four Grand Prixs and the world championship in 1962.

One of the first passenger cars Hill ever owned was a 1929 Austin. It cost him $70. It was so beat-up that parts kept falling off en route. The brake functioned only sometimes. Hill, being penniless, replaced nothing. He used to stop the car by scrubbing its tire walls against curbs.

Hill advises all would-be racing drivers to acquire a similar car. "The chief qualities of a racing driver are concentration, determination, and anticipation," he says. "A 1929 Austin without brakes develops all three—anticipation rather more than the first two, perhaps. Nothing better."

Jim
Clark:

"I'M NOT CONVINCED I am the best driver," said Jim Clark. "I never set out with any ambition to be world champion. I enjoyed racing. I enjoy it still. My goal was to enjoy racing and to win each race if I could. That's all. I never hoped or expected to be world champion."

Clark, saying this, had just won his first world championship. He had won seven of ten world championship races, a record, and nineteen of twenty-nine road races overall that 1963 season. He also entered three track races in America, winning at Milwaukee, finishing second at Indianapolis, and breaking down at Trenton. In America alone he won about $70,000. It was a season such as no other driver had ever had before him, and none is soon likely to have again. He was twenty-seven years old.

"I had to be coaxed into my first Grand Prix car," Clark said. "In 1959, Reg Parnell, who was then team manager for Aston Martin, offered me a car for 1960. I sort of shuddered and cried, 'help'. I told him I didn't think I could handle it."

Clark's modesty seems so deeply ingrained that some people are suspicious of it. "If you ask me," Graham Hill remarked once, "the whole thing is an act." But on further reflection, Hill was moved to say: "It may be as Jimmy says that he is puzzled to see how he has got this far. He's got a terrific car after all. He may wonder how much of it is due to the car and how much to himself. I think that if I were in his place I'd be a bit puzzled, wondering if what everybody was saying was true."

Stirling Moss explains Clark's seemingly excessive modesty by saying: "You must remember that Jimmy is very immature for his age. He is from the country after all. Every place in Scotland is the backwoods, but Jimmy is not even from a city, he was raised on a farm, and so he is more immature than another person his age would be. He is not sure of himself yet." Moss felt that

Clark, not being at ease as a world champion, as a celebrity, not really knowing how to behave, still behaved as he was taught to behave in school.

CLARK was born March 4, 1936, in Kilmany, Scotland, the fifth child and first son of a prosperous landowner. He was sent to boarding schools from the age of ten to sixteen. His schoolwork was mediocre and he played all the games boys play, particularly rugby. Once he tore ligaments in his leg and was in a cast eight weeks. This is the only injury Clark has ever had. He has crashed some race cars since, but has never been scratched.

After he finished school at sixteen, Clark went to work for his father, caring for the herds of his father's prize sheep. He had learned to back the family car down the driveway at ten; at seventeen he got his first car, a Sunbeam Talbot. His father bought a new car and now for the first time the old one was not traded in; it went to Jimmy. Jimmy had always liked fast driving, he had a feel for it, and he soon entered the Sunbeam Talbot in rallies and events close to home. He was so good that people began lending him faster cars, and he won forty-five sports car races in the next few years.

On Boxing Day 1959 Clark raced a Lotus Elite at Brands Hatch. It was a short race, and Clark nearly won it, being nipped at the finish by Colin Chapman in an identical car. In those days Chapman not only built the Lotuses, but raced them too. Chapman was on the lookout for drivers, and Clark had caught his eye.

Meanwhile, Reg Parnell had offered the Aston Martin Grand Prix car for 1960, and Clark, who is nothing if not a dutiful son, was worried about what his father would say if he accepted Parnell's offer and went into racing full time.

Clark recalls: "Here I was supposed to be running a farm, Dad had his own farm to look after, and I was away half the time racing. He used to say to me, 'a fine thing this hobby of yours has developed into. You're spending all your time on it and it's not paying you back a thing.'

"I said, 'Dad, it can pay me a very good living if you'll let it.'

"Then I called Aston Martin and told Reg Parnell that if he wanted me, he'd better come up to Scotland and talk to my father. He came up, and convinced my father that this thing was worth a try."

But Aston Martin soon abandoned the sport. Clark then accepted an offer from Chapman to become fourth man on the three car Lotus team. However, the third man, Alan Stacey, was soon killed, and Clark had a car in nearly every race that year. The next year he was second man, the team leader being Innes Ireland. Ireland won a lot of races, he was a fast, experienced man, but at the end of the season Chapman dropped him and installed Clark as No. 1.

"Even in 1961 Clark was faster than Ireland," recalls Chapman. "It may not have shown, because being No. 1, Ireland always had the better car, but I was satisfied that Clark was the faster." Satisfied enough to drop a winning driver for one who was virtually untried. Clark's amazing natural talent was and always has been this obvious.

Clark cannot say why or how he drives a car faster than others. Moss says Clark's skill is instinctive, that he has learned very little since he started to race, that he had his great gift for speed from the beginning. This may be the truth. In September 1959 Clark was offered a Jaguar in the Tourist Trophy sports car race. His co-driver was to be the American, Masten Gregory. Gregory, a member of the Cooper Grand Prix team, had been racing steadily in Europe for six seasons. He was fast and experienced.

"To me, Masten was a god," recalls Clark. "I hardly dared talk to him." Clark at this time had hardly ever been out of Scotland, but halfway through the first practice session he found that he was lapping much faster than Gregory. "I was absolutely astonished," Clark says.

CLARK has no close friend (he says) among the other drivers. He loves his farm (1200 acres, 500 cattle, 2500 sheep) and the country life, but he loves racing too. Or at least he loves getting into a race car and driving like the wind, which may not be the same thing. There have been drivers like Moss who loved everything about racing, and others who enjoyed the sidelines and adulation but disliked, or perhaps feared, the racing. Clark is the only one I know who seems to like the racing only. And already he knows that he can never be happy again just farming. When he can't race any longer, he will have to find something to take its place. He is worried about this already. He is really a very serious young man. He laughs often and has a gorgeous smile, but he doesn't contribute any jokes or sparkling conversation himself, and sometimes he seems rather too serious, too humorless.

He is small, five feet seven inches tall, the same size as Moss, though for some reason he always appears much taller than this. He hates smoking and smoke-filled rooms, but is too well-mannered to complain when others blow smoke in his face. He dislikes drinking, but will sip at a drink in company, if this seems necessary. He likes light music and jazz, photography, water skiing, and dancing. He hates girls in heavy makeup, dark sunglasses, or dyed hair. He loves hunting and the loneliness of the country around his farm.

In 1964, world champion and importuned on all sides, he was often testy to reporters and sometimes rude. But he almost always had a smile for fans. He feels obliged to make speeches and appearances whenever asked to do so, and he answers all his mail, often a hundred letters a week. He doesn't enjoy this, but he does it. Fans demand autographed photos, so Clark sends them out. He buys the photos and pays the secretaries himself, although other drivers get the photos printed up by Esso or some other sponsor. Clark would not think of asking Esso (or anyone else) for a favor. Moss was surprised that Clark had never asked Moss's advice on conducting the business sidelines of motor racing. Moss had gone through all this years ago, and no one had ever exploited the sport as Moss did. "You would have thought Jimmy would ask me what to do at one time or another," Moss remarked once. "I would have been glad to tell him, of course."

When Clark heard this, he was surprised. "Why should I ask Moss' advice about business?" he said. "I never asked him how to drive a car." Had Clark ever asked advice on race driving? "No, never."

When he wanted advice on incorporating himself, he went to both a lawyer and an accountant. He paid them. "I never asked anyone for anything," Clark says. "I never even asked anyone to give me a drive." It is normal for young drivers to beg owners for drives. Clark never did this once.

"Does this sound stubborn of me? I don't like to ask people for things. They might not want to give what I ask for, and that would be awkward."

Clark hates awkwardness, hates being under an obligation to anyone. Right from the start he was by far the best driver, whatever company he competed in. So right from the start, people offered him cars to drive. If he had been less fast, no one would have offered the cars, and it seems likely that Clark never would have bent his pride enough actually to request a ride. Thus the world would never have heard of him.

CLARK FEELS that four principal elements enter into race driving: concentration, accuracy, resistance to fatigue, and icy nerve. For him, the first is the toughest ("I would have to remind myself all the time to concentrate") and the last he would prefer to discount. He does not like all this talk of nerve and death. "Look at me, you can't say I am a man of icy nerve. I am actually a very nervous person, I bite my nails all the way down, I fidget all the time." This is true, but not the same thing. Icy nerve in a race car is closing off your mind to the possibility of disaster, and this Clark obviously has no trouble with.

"I realize the danger is there, of course," Clark says. "When I get away with something, I say to myself: 'Christ, that's getting a bit close.'" Near misses have no other effect on him. He is not a brooder, either before or after.

Ricardo Rodriguez:

RICARDO RODRIGUEZ was motorcycle champion of Mexico at thirteen. At fourteen he quit the sport because it seemed kid stuff. He became a racing driver at fifteen, sharing sports cars with his brother, Pedro, two years older.

The boys raced all over the world in hot cars provided by Papa Rodriguez, in his fifties, a portly, wealthy man and friend of politicians. Before a race the boys would sometimes kneel on the tarmac to be blessed by their young mother. Then they would race while Papa cheered them on and Mama sat calmly in the shade reading a book.

Papa entered the boys everywhere. He would get furious when Ricardo's entry was rejected (as happened at Le Mans) on the grounds that Ricardo was not a racing driver, he was a child.

Ricardo made the Ferrari team at nineteen. He looked even younger and adults around him were always telling him when to put on or take off sweaters, and not to drink so much soda pop. Papa Rodriguez exulted in Ricardo's progress. He said he had been spending $80,000 a year on cars for his boys, but it was worth it. He predicted proudly that Ricardo would be world champion almost at once.

Ricardo had more nerve than skill, more ambition than experience. Some rivals thought he had great talent, some did not. Phil Hill said, "If he lives, I'll be surprised."

Ricardo was such a hero in Mexico that a Mexican Grand Prix was organized for the first time in November 1962. The mob felt sure Ricardo would win it. But he was killed during practice the first afternoon, almost as soon as practice opened—in his own backyard so to speak.

Dan Gurney:

SON OF AN opera singer, Dan Gurney went to two junior colleges in California and was graduated from both. Once he considered buying a motorcycle, but as the owner of the machine remembers: "He didn't really look like a motorcycle-type boy. He was very clean-cut and nice looking."

In Riverside, Gurney belonged to the hot rod set. At night in souped-up cars, he and his pals would race through half-finished, deserted subdivisions at the edge of the city.

From about 1954, when he got out of the army, all Gurney ever wanted to be was a racing driver. All the police ever wanted to do was stop Gurney and his pals from practicing in the public streets at night. The boys took to running their impromptu races without lights. The police sneaked up on them in beat-up old panel trucks, or swooped down on paired motorcycles which, at a distance, looked like an oncoming car.

Gurney collected many speeding tickets. The few jobs he held bored him. He began to win sports car races in California, he got married and had two children, and then a Ferrari dealer in New York, Luigi Chinetti, offered him a car at Le Mans. He was fast at Le Mans and soon Ferrari gave him a try-out at Modena, followed by the usual non-lucrative Ferrari contract.

In 1959, age twenty-eight, Gurney kissed his wife and kids goodbye, betting the packet, and came to Europe as a Ferrari team driver, salary $160 per month, and not a single race entry guaranteed.

He crashed a Ferrari in practice. It turned over but did not hurt him. He was given a few drives, did fairly well, and then when Jean Behra was fired, Gurney took Behra's seat, earning about $7,000 that first summer. The next year his wife and children came to Europe with him.

He now raced for BRM. His machine hurtled off the road in the Dutch Grand Prix, chopped up a spectator, and landed upside down with Gurney in it.

Gurney watched them cover the dead man. "This is a cruel sport," he said.

He had a broken arm and torn rib cartilages. Worse, he had no further confidence in the BRM. He raced on, ignoring the pain of his ribs, using the broken arm as he had to, but he did not race too fast anymore. I wrote an article about what Gurney had been through, wondering if he still wanted to go on with "the cruel sport."

Gurney, reading this, was furious. Friends told me he talked of suing. He felt I had questioned his courage, but I didn't mean to. A husband and father who was not an idiot, who had known fright and suffering, who had seen others killed around him, might never be able to hold his foot down again. He might be unable to through nerves; he might not want to, knowing now the fragility of the machine and of himself. The decision he had to make was not between courage and cowardice; he had to decide if the prize was worth the price. To throw in his hand would not be cowardice. Nor would the opposite, to me, prove courage.

Angry as he was, Gurney never said a word to me. He was not warm as before, but he was always polite. I always respected him for what this effort cost him. I respect him too, because he hung on for nearly a year in a car he hated, waiting for his arm to heal, waiting for his mind to heal so that he could decide what he wanted to do.

Gurney is today one of the four or five drivers who gives everything he has in every race; and he is one of the four or five fastest too. He has said that a major problem has been to prevent praise and success from causing him to drive rashly. "You must continually ask yourself," he says, "*Am I being brave or merely foolish?* Every time you put your foot down, you must ask yourself."

He has four children now. He seems to love motor racing more than ever. He is also more and more tense, more and more deliberate in his movements and his thoughts.

Richie Ginther:

BEFORE HE HAD done any real racing himself, Ginther rode twice with Phil Hill in the Carrera Pan Americana road race up the spine of Mexico. Once they finished second, once they went off a cliff and tumbled downhill in dust and noise.

Hill did all the driving. Ginther so trusted Hill that he wasn't even scared, he said.

Now he was known in motor racing as "the man who rode with Phil Hill in the Pan-American." This, Ginther says, got very tiring. Through Hill, Ginther met other racing people, and soon found himself a Ferrari sales dealer on the West Coast. This necessitated several trips to the Ferrari factory.

By 1960, the strain of balancing profit and loss had made a nervous wreck out of Ginther. At twenty-nine, he quit, devoted himself to racing sports cars in California, then was asked by Ferrari to come to Italy as a test driver at about $160 per month.

Olivier Gendebien:

AN ANCESTOR of Olivier Gendebien helped found Belgium. Gendebien is heir to the baronetcy. He need never work, but, from 1948 to 1952 he cleared roads and leveled forests in the Belgian Congo, hunting buffalo in his spare time.

Returning to Belgium, he heard of a local car race, was curious to enter, but had no car. He found a man who owned a stout looking convertible, and the chap was willing to rent the car out for an equally stout sum of money. "But if you ruin my car, it will cost you four times as much," the man shouted after him.

Gendebien worried only about denting his rented car. He motored along at the edge of the road, waved by car after car. Not surprisingly, he finished last.

No one watching spied a future champion. No one remarked on any great skill or brilliant reactions. No one supposed he would later win Le Mans four times, the Targa Florio and Sebring three times each, and class victories in the Mille Miglia twice.

In 1956 in pouring rain, Gendebien won the Mille Miglia (Grand Turismo Class), having slid and skidded through villages and mountains for eleven hours. He had bounced off walls, curbs, and earthen embankments, and all the fenders were dented or torn. When he climbed from the battered car, he was badly shaken. "I did not know," he said, "that at thirty-one a man could be such a fool."

Joakim Bonnier:

JO BONNIER was sent to Oxford to study English, and then to Paris "to do something in our family publishing firm." Bonnier was never quite sure what, so after a time he went back to Stockholm and began selling Alfa Romeo cars.

To attract attention to his dealership, he began to race the cars he was selling. There were a lot of crackups: "you have all that enthusiasm and no experience."

He had his first serious crash in a sports car race at Imola, Italy, in 1956. He was twenty-six. "Somebody got in my way and I flipped. I was flung into a telegraph post head on. I was asleep for some time."

Bonnier had three vertebrae and several ribs fractured, but he flew to Rome and competed in three races. "I felt that with luck I might get on the Maserati team for 1957. If I could just make some kind of showing at Rome . . ."

Hurt, sometimes dizzy, he finished sixth, fourth, and first. Maserati hired him.

Jackie Stewart:

WHEN HE awoke beside his wife, Helen, in the Annette et Lubin hotel in Spa on the morning of the 1966 Belgian Grand Prix, Jackie Stewart could hear from bed that it was raining. He went to peer out the window.

The day before he had qualified his BRM second fastest at 141 miles per hour. Now he ordered breakfast sent up, and while waiting he and Helen talked about the future. About the house they meant to buy, with six bedrooms to accommodate the big family they planned on. About the schools they would send their son to, their first child—he was seven months old. They did not talk about the rain, or about the race to come, which, if the road were dry, would be the fastest road race of all time. If wet it would be slower. Either way, it would be dangerous.

A little later Helen went down to lunch. Jackie lay in bed until she had gone out, then rose and put on his racing clothes.

In the restaurant he sat beside Helen, but did not eat. He wasn't hungry.

At 1:30, two hours before the race, he started out to the circuit, seven miles away, in his rented Volkswagen. The afternoon was dark but dry. The bucolic countryside passed by. Stewart was not worried about the possibility of rain, he said, and seemed only slightly nervous about the race in general. He told of races he had won in the rain. "In the rain you really have to get the feel of things."

Of course one of his only two crashes had been in the rain too.

At the circuit Stewart entered the official parking lot and squeezed into a slot. Kids thrust programs through the window and he signed them. Then he rolled the window up for privacy and went through his satchel, discarding three sets of goggles and affixing a green tinted visor to his helmet, for the sky really looked like rain now.

Tony Rudd, designer of the BRMs, came up. Stewart rolled down the window.

"You'll be on your auxiliary tank for one lap at the end," Rudd said. "We'll signal you."

A few minutes later Stewart crouched in his dark green BRM, eyes glued to the starter's flag. The afternoon was still dry, though darker than ever. The flag whipped down and Jackie Stewart surged off the line, engine screaming. As the cars roared down into the valley, then up the steep, curving hill opposite, he was second or third. There was too much smoke to tell for sure.

Two minutes later and four miles away, at a point halfway down the Masta straight, a rain squall came down. Stewart, making 150 miles per hour—perhaps more—saw the squall ahead and did not lift his foot. Or if he did lift it, he did not lift it enough.

Inside the rain Stewart could not see, could not steer, and when he tried desperate, gentle braking there was a centimeter of water between his tires and the road—the car was aquaplaning, and it spun wildly round and round, hurtling down the road sideways, backwards, sideways again at tremendous speed.

Halfway along the Masta straight there is a kink, and when the out-of-control BRM reached this kink, it plowed off into the scenery and began to hit things. Both front wheels were sheared off. The side of the car walloped a low brick wall over a culvert. This staved in the side of the car, and broke Stewart's collarbone. It also ruptured the fuel tank on that side, bathing him in gasoline. The car dropped nine feet into the bottom of a concrete driveway beside a barn. And came to rest.

The storm moved over the speeding race cars, embracing all of them, wrecking seven. Seven others got through, including the Ferrari of John Surtees which was to win the race, though at an average speed of only 114 miles per hour.

Meanwhile the rain pelted down on Stewart in his crushed car. The cockpit was the equivalent of a basin. He was up to his hips in gasoline, and the part of him still

conscious was terrified of fire. Graham Hill and Bob Bondurant, who had crashed closest to him, dragged him out of the wreckage, carried him into the barn and laid him on a bed of hay. His skin was being scalded by the racing fuel with its additives, and Hill stripped him of his racing coveralls, but not of his fireproof long-johns, which were also fuel saturated. Stewart was squirming with pain. They waited half an hour for the ambulance to find them.

TO STEWART this accident proved that it was much more difficult to kill a modern racing driver than it used to be. The driver's reclining position tends to dissipate forces over his entire body, he said later. The new cars are so tight around him that it is almost impossible to get thrown out, and the airplane-wing-type construction is much, much tougher than the old tubular steel frame.

"I'm very safety conscious, as you may have noticed," Stewart had remarked a few hours before the race. He had just instructed his mechanics to reinforce his roll bar, and to install safety belts. Only a few years ago drivers had wanted to be thrown out of the car in case of accident, for they feared fire most of all. Now it is all changed. A driver wants to stay in the machine, and he wears all that fireproof clothing. Stewart also wears a bandanna type face mask and is having fireproof gloves made. Describing this, he checked his wrist watch's second hand and said: "Of course wearing all that you sweat a lot, but that's not important, for in case of fire you should be safe for thirty seconds, and by then somebody should be able to get you out."

He checked his watch again: "There, thirty seconds. Quite a long time, actually."

Stewart seemed to be pretending that due to modern science a driver had become immortal. No one had yet been killed in a monocoque car in Europe. But his crash in Belgium proved the opposite, if it proved anything. It was ten to fifteen minutes before Hill and Bondurant could pry him loose from the wreck, and he was so soaked in fuel that later, lying naked on a table in an emergency room, he begged the nurses to "wash me all over." He merely was lucky that the crash happened on the first lap and

in pouring rain so that nothing on the car was hot enough to start the blaze that might have consumed him.

THE BELGIAN crash seemed to prove that Stewart is not only the new face and voice that Grand Prix racing has so desperately needed in this era of silent, brilliant but basically faceless men such as Jim Clark, Graham Hill, Surtees, and others; but also that in addition to his charm, his eloquence, his blinding intelligence, he is more fearless than they. Or more ambitions, perhaps. But it is the same thing. No one else has ever come so far so fast in the sport, nor talks as plainly about how far he intends to go and how much money he intends to earn.

Jim Clark, whom Stewart resembles in so many ways, did not win a world championship race until his third season. Stewart won one (the Italian Grand Prix) last year, his first season in the Formula One cars, was second in three others, and third behind Clark and Hill on the season. Last winter Stewart went to Australia and New Zealand and in eight races was first four times, second and fourth, and twice retired, once while in the lead. Clark and Hill were there too, but could not stay with Stewart most of the time. Hill won two races, and Clark only one.

"Jackie's riding the crest of a wave," says Hill thoughtfully. "He's got a lot of confidence." Hill is in the peculiar position of being ten years older, a former world champion, the titular leader of the two-car BRM team—and possibly not as fast as the new boy wonder.

All of the drivers will tell you that the five fastest—indeed the only five really fast Grand Prix drivers—are Clark, Hill, Surtees, Dan Gurney, and Stewart. A year ago none of the others had ever heard Stewart's name.

Stewart says flatly: "Jimmy's fastest. The other four of us are about the same."

Richie Ginther, driving for Cooper this year, says: "Stewart's faster than Graham, and Graham must be really burning."

There is no hostility between Hill and Stewart. They seem fond of each other, and Hill seems to look after Stewart to some extent. And of course he probably saved

Stewart's life in the Belgian crash. But two weeks before that in Monte Carlo Stewart won the race handily and Graham Hill, running third with a disintegrating clutch, was trying so hard to catch him that he spun out and nearly crashed. At Indianapolis a week after that, it was Stewart who led the race until the 190th of 200 laps, and who got a standing ovation when he pushed his broken car into the pits, leaving victory to Hill, who was regarded as having lucked in.

Hill will tell you that he is team leader, and that if he and Stewart are in the lead in a race, and there is a gap behind them, he will slow down to save the car and Stewart will do likewise, and Hill will win the race. But in fact this situation did occur in the Italian Grand Prix, and Stewart did not drop back, though he admits "I did not know what the hell to do out there." And again on the final lap Hill tried so hard to pass him that Hill momentarily lost control, leaving Stewart to win by three seconds.

"This year," says Stewart, "we are equals, and I'd be trying just as hard to win as Graham."

"Jackie is so fast," says Hill, "because he is a natural athlete, he has competitive spirit, and he has had the opportunity to get into good cars early in his career."

Hill himself has never been called a natural driver, which is what everyone calls Clark, and now Stewart. "Jackie is I suppose like me in one respect," says Clark, "in that nobody ever had to teach him very much about driving a race car."

But Clark and Stewart both fell into top cars right at the start of their careers, whereas Hill's first four years were spent driving dogs: "I had no money, no contacts." But he would hustle in every race. "Everyone could see I was trying, but when you're in a situation like that, nobody says you're a natural. The bloke out front's the natural."

Now it irks him that Clark and Stewart are called naturals, while he himself is called a pusher, or fiercely combative or some such thing (as are Surtees and Gurney also), and the competition is usually conceded to the naturals in advance by the press and most spectators.

And although Hill attempts to mask all emotion when he speaks of Stewart, some seems to shine through. "Jackie's very keen financially," says Hill. "He's got a good eye for the baubies. That's a Scottish word. It means money. Mercenary is perhaps too strong a word, but he knows his value. He's very astute, very ambitious. He's got an eye for publicity." Hill himself disapproves of publicity. "A man has his own standards and his own attitude. I can't change my nature. I have a lot of friends in motor racing, and if I sought publicity I would have less." Hill rarely seeks to merchandise himself; Stewart brags about having made more money already than any other driver ever in equivalent time. "I don't know how he can be so sure of that," mutters Hill.

The aloofness of Hill keeps reporters at a distance, although once you break through to him he is, and always has been, funny and charming. The rest of the fast drivers, Clark, Surtees, and Gurney, are similarly difficult to approach. At a time when the shape of the race cars dropped the drivers so deep inside that their faces could barely be seen by the crowds, a breed of drivers grew up who did not care about being invisible in the cars and silent out of them. Now along has come Stewart, who always has something to say.

About being compared to Jim Clark: "They used to talk about me as the new Jim Clark, but they don't compare us anymore. They just talk about 'those two bloody Scots.'"

About breaking down at Indianapolis when far in the lead: "I've worked it all out and I've decided it wasn't important—it was only $150,000."

At Indianapolis the caution light came on early. "I thought: some clown has stuffed it into the wall. When we came around there were flags everywhere, and garbage all over the road. I went looking for Jimmy, and he for me, and then we both went looking for Graham to see that he was all right." Later Clark spun out just in front of him. "I was making about 150 miles per hour, but he was too, backwards. The speed differential was not that much and it was like going by in slow motion and I wagged my finger at him as if to say 'naughty, naughty.' You should have seen the expression on Jimmy's face."

Stewart believes that the day of the European driver has dawned at Indianapolis, that the traditional Indy, dirty-fingered-type driver is finished because such men lack sensitivity. They could drive the old roadsters, which were insensitive cars, on brute strength and bravery—all such cars required. But it takes delicacy and finesse to drive the lighter, more responsive, more agile rear-engine cars which have now come in. Such cars can be driven through corners on a variety of lines rather than only one, and can move around other cars in traffic. Stewart believes that Europe produces more intelligent drivers because the sport is so socially accepted in Europe. High class young men go into it. He believes that Indy must now work hard to acquire such an image itself. "The A. J. Foyts were good for American racing for a while, but they are hurting it now." Stewart found to his disgust that most Indy drivers did not know how to express themselves, and that at the prize giving ceremony, some of them were chewing gum.

Stewart's wife Helen, who had been listening to him, spellbound, said: "He's fascinating, isn't he? He's always been that way. I've known Jackie since I was sixteen, and even then I used to sit listening to him with my mouth open, he was that fascinating."

STEWART was born John Young Stewart on June 11, 1939, about fifty yards from the modest bungalow where he lives today, about twelve miles from Glasgow. His father owned a garage business and auto agency, and ten years ago an older brother named Jimmy raced cars successfully until crashes at Le Mans and the Nürburgring ruined one of his arms. When Jackie drifted into racing in 1961 at the age of twenty-two, it was under the *nom de guerre* of A. N. Other, because he did not want to upset his mother.

He had finished school at fifteen, as is normal in Britain, but did not stop learning. He worked for his father and learned the agency and garage business, and he incessantly questioned people who knew something he wished to know himself. One of the bizarre aspects of interviewing this young man is his way of interviewing the interviewer right back. He will answer your questions for a while, but then you have to answer his.

He keeps his eyes open, reads a lot, and he collects books on subjects that interest him. Though he drinks Coca-Cola almost exclusively, he owns shelves full of wine books that he plans to read soon: "Wine is one of the things I want to know about, but I don't have time. I don't have a weekend off this year until November."

Stewart raced only three times in 1961, five in 1962, twenty-three in 1963 when he won fourteen races, and set a lap record at Charterhall, Britain, four miles per hour faster that Jim Clark had ever made there. "It was obvious right away how good he was," says Colin Chapman, owner-designer of Lotus. "There were signs. Consistency, his attitude, the speed with which he learned a circuit—and remembered it."

In March 1964 Stewart was offered a test drive by Ken Tyrell who was running the official Cooper Formula III team. Bruce McLaren, a driver with seven years of Grand Prix experience, tested the car first. Then Stewart got in. It was the first time he'd ever driven a single-seater car, a car "made to motor race," as he put it, and he went quicker than McLaren who, until then, "had been like a god" to him. Offers to drive poured in, and Stewart ran fifty-three races that year, winning twenty-eight. By Christmas he was driving a Lotus team car in South Africa. He won one heat and broke down in the other.

Explaining Stewart's quick success, Dan Gurney says "He's raced a lot of miles. A lot of guys don't run in three years what he ran in one." Ginther suggests that Stewart was able to make a lot of people like him and offer him rides; that Stewart was as versatile as Clark at handling many types of cars, and as good a politician as Graham Hill at getting owners and mechanics to work for him. In Stewart, adds Ginther, "Graham has really met his match."

STEWART IS slightly taller than Clark, 5 feet 8, but has heavily muscled shoulders and weighs 154. He has a strong Scottish accent, whereas Clark has a neutral, upper class British accent. Stewart has smallish eyes which crinkle into a winning smile, but which at other times tend to make him look sleepy, which he is not.

From the start he set a high price on his services, and wouldn't come down, and when he recently rejected a contract offer from Dunlop Rubber, they wound up paying him two and a half times as much. He draws $1,260 starting money per Grand Prix race: "I don't call that a very good deal, do you?" But he gets retainers from Dunlop, Shell, and BRM, and makes his own deals for other races. He would not go to Indianapolis until John Mecom Jr. paid him heavily: "I don't care whether I race for Mecom or the president of the United States, I'm a professional and I expect to be paid a fee, win or lose." He has taken over his father's business, has spread himself into five companies in all, and now shares Clark's lawyer and accountant, crowing that these men probably made mistakes when they started with Clark, which they no longer make, and this will save Jackie Stewart plenty of money. Stewart won over $25,000 at Indianapolis, and may earn as much as $100,000 this year: "The way I see it, I'm a young businessman who is about to make a great deal of money."

Clark, starting out, asked advice from no one, but Stewart, who calls Clark his closest friend in racing, went straight to Clark. "I imagine I was a bit of a pest at first." Clark gave him warnings at certain new circuits, such as places where puddles collect in the rain, or breaking distances, or corners where the verge is soft and a driver had best not let his wheels go off the road.

Clark says he cannot explain why Stewart is so fast. Stewart himself says: "I haven't a clue. I don't know anything about my car, I just get in it and drive it."

Which brings us back to Stewart's fearlessness.

There are two types of fearlessness, the moral (or emotional or intellectual, or whatever) kind; and the physical kind.

When he had that first drive in Ken Tyrell's Formula III Cooper, and beat McLaren's time, Tyrell offered to be his manager, to pay him $8,400 immediately in return for ten percent of Stewart's earnings over the next three years.

Stewart at this time was newly married, and flat broke: "I didn't have fifty pounds to my name."

Stewart thought the offer over, then rejected it.

"Ken Tyrell was a pretty switched-on bloke," explains Stewart today. "I figured that if he believed in me to that extent, I must have a future, and that if I could stand the poverty just a little bit longer, it would be worth a lot more than $8,400."

As for physical fearlessness, Stewart will tell you that he hates racing on the Nürburgring, the fourteen-mile, 175-curve circuit through the Eifel Mountains west of Bonn. "It's bloody terrifying," he says. "Take the Fuchsroehre. You go down there the first time in fourth gear and you say to yourself that you ought to be able to do it in sixth gear flat out, so the next time around you go down that hill in sixth at 163 miles an hour, switching back and forth from one side of the road to the other, the trees and hedges going by in such a hurry that you can't see anything but greenery, and you think, Christ, I'm going too fast, I'm not going to have enough time to do everything. The car is leaping about, and every time it leaves the ground you have to put a bit of a lock on it so it will be pointing the right way when it comes down, and then in the dip at the bottom of the hill the g forces are tremendous, you're squashed down in your seat, the suspension isn't working, and you realize you can't control the car anymore, it's going to take its own line up the hill and you wonder what that line will be, and you can't even get your foot off the accelerator and onto the brake accurately, you probably only get a corner of it, and the car goes up that hill like on tram tracks, and you can't steer it, and you wonder where it's going to go, all the time trying to come down two gears and get it slowed enough to get around the left-hander, then the right, left, right coming up next—I tell you it's bloody terrifying.

"But the second time you do it, you know that the line it's going to take up the hill is all right, and your mind and body are synchronized to the elements you're competing against, and it is all so clear to you, it seems to happen in slow motion.

"It won't terrify you again until the next year when there have been some improvements to the car and tires, and you go down there a little bit faster."

Part Two:

The Machines

The Shape of Speed

THE ULTIMATE race cars of the past are in museums now; fathers troop by trying to explain to children how it was. But the children don't believe, because the old cars just don't look fast anymore. No car of its day could beat the 1939 Mercedes-Benz (opposite page), but the new, knife-smooth Lotus would leave it behind.

The shape of speed changes relentlessly. Soon the Lotus will be in a museum too, and other fathers will troop by, trying to explain to other children, who also won't believe.

Close Fit:

LAST OF THE front-engined cars: Sometimes called the most beautiful race car ever, the 1959 BRM, above left, won only one race. Ditto the bulky 1960 Ferrari. These were roomy cars. The cockpit was something a driver could rattle around in. Carroll Shelby's 1959 Aston Martin, above, was too fat even then, but was not hopelessly outclassed. But by 1962 every car was low, flat, and rear-engined, and the driver wore the cockpit around his neck like a collar. Shoulder movement was constricted by the narrow cockpit walls, and the driver's chin was lower than the Plexiglas necklace of the wraparound windscreen. Graham Hill's cockpit, too narrow at the beginning of the season, had to be widened to let the driver in at all. The next year a kind of ultimate was reached in Bruce McLaren's Cooper, right. The cockpit closes in so tightly that the driver almost cannot turn his head.

Lower, Thinner, Faster . . . Faster!

WHEN CAR RACING started in 1894, the machines were as high as a horse, and a man needed help to climb up onto one. Today the machines are lower than the height of their own tires, but are so tight and narrow that the driver still may need help getting in or out.

In most cases the driver must step over the cowling onto his seat, then slither and wriggle under the steering wheel until his feet are on the pedals. Now the driver is virtually lying down, legs fully outstretched on the pedals, arms fully outstretched to reach the wheel and gear lever. His chin rests on his chest. Otherwise, he wouldn't be able to see the road.

All Grand Prix machines are, by regulation, limited to 1.5-liter engines and a minimum weight of 450 kilograms (990 pounds). This leaves only two basic ways to produce a faster car: squeeze a few extra horsepower out of your engine, which is the same size as his, or reduce your car's frontal area (and wind resistance) more than the other man believes possible. Minor improvements can be made in braking, road holding, and gear ratios; but more horsepower and/or less frontal area is all that will help flat-out speed.

So the cars get lower and lower, thinner and thinner—and faster and faster.

Some marques could work on both engine and wind resistance, but Colin Chapman, who owns Lotus, buys his engines ready made from Coventry-Climax. He couldn't work on beefing up engines. For Lotus, lower wind resistance was the only hope.

And so the 1962 Lotus (right), which Chapman and his staff designed, had no tubular frame. It was, in effect, two four-foot-long gas tanks connected by a thin undershield. This formed a kind of tub, with the engine bolted to one end, and the front wheel assembly bolted to the other.

The driver reclined in his tub on a pad. This was the first monocoque racing car ever built, and it is an idea which was first thought of for the wings of airplanes. The gas tanks which formed the seat (or bed, if you prefer) held twenty-six gallons. They were built of what airplane designers call stressed skin. The effect is extremely rigid. According to Chapman, this gave a tremendous advantage on very fast, sweeping curves on circuits like Spa and Reims. When these curves are taken at speeds above 130 miles per hour, the car's frame tends to bend slightly, regaining shape on the straight. Chapman's cars, presumably, did not lose shape at all.

But this was an incidental advantage. The main one was that the car, minus any frame, was narrower and lower than any other. The car rode 3.75 inches off the road. The gear lever was at arm's length, and the sides of the cowling, curving in, were so tight the driver could not bend his arm properly to shift. This, conceded Chapman, was a problem. Under the front cowling, the driver's legs were tight together. He could barely bend his knees to work the pedals.

In any case, in a three-hour race, most drivers are now so tightly enclosed that they cannot even squirm, much less change position to relieve stiffness or cramps. However, most drivers say this is preferable to being tossed all over the cockpit in every corner.

All the British cars—BRM, Cooper, Lotus, Lola, Brabham—are extremely low and narrow. This design lead is understandable. Only BRM makes its own engine and could search for extra horsepower. The others, buying engines from Coventry-Climax, could search only for less wind resistance. About 1955 this took the form of placing engines behind the driver for the sole purpose of making a lower line. In the thirties, the German Auto-Union was a rear-engined racing car—a huge, ponderous one; the engine was in the back for balance, not for line. But now, with Cooper leading the way, the British began lowering and thinning their cars. The result is the slender, snug, modern racer.

At the Nürburgring before the 1962 German Grand Prix, Hermann Lang did one lap in the 1939 Mercedes-Benz in which he won the European championship that year. Lang and the big Mercedes made a lap record

there twenty-three years ago. It was nine minutes, forty-seven seconds. In 1962 Clark's Lotus nipped around about a minute faster.

The Nürburgring is virtually unchanged since 1939. Lang had changed. One lap left him sweating and tired. He was baldish, plump, and past fifty. And, of course, race cars have changed.

The heavy Mercedes swallowed Lang up; Clark is nearly as big as his car. But the difference is more than size. The Lotus has better acceleration, smoother suspension, far more efficient brakes, and synthetic tires perhaps ten times more adherent than Lang's rubber ones.

Lang's car could do 195 miles per hour on the straight at the Nürburgring, and over 200 elsewhere. Its supercharged engine was two yards long, developed over 465 horsepower and devoured two tankloads of gas in every race.

Clark's car is 1,700 pounds lighter, and its engine develops only about a third as much horsepower. It never refuels during races. It can make only about 160 miles per hour flat out. On the straight, the Mercedes would overwhelm it. But for a simple bend, Lang would have to slow down to 20 miles per hour—while Clark sped around at 65.

Anyway, no one was racing Lang that day. He came down the straight extremely fast, the car bounding as if it were out of control, the enormous thunderous roar of those 465 horses overpowering everything. Such colossal, thrilling noise does not exist in car racing anymore, though all modern cars lap much faster. Old-timers talk about that noise, those great bounding cars, all the time. They long for their return.

It would be nice, but then they wouldn't win races.

Part Three:

The Factories

Ferrari Automobili

THERE ARE NO ROADS where cars are raced which have not known the banshee wail and frightening agility of Ferrari race cars. Ferraris have sped to victory in Florida, Venezuela, and Australia, through the forests of West Germany, the streets of Monte Carlo, the mountains of Mexico, the deserts of North Africa. They have won races lasting two hours and races lasting seven days. Ferrari drivers have won five world championships since 1952; in the nine seasons that the sports car world championship existed, Ferrari won it seven times.

No other marque can match the record in victories of the blood-red cars. Nor their record in death.

In 1953 in Argentina, a Ferrari slewed into the mob, slaughtered about fifteen, and maimed many more.

In Italy during the 1957 Mille Miglia, a Ferrari rocketed off the road and killed eleven.

In Cuba during the 1958 Gran Premio, a Ferrari killed seven.

At Monza, Italy, during the 1961 Grand Prix, a Ferrari killed sixteen.

Six drivers under contract to the Ferrari factory, skilled professionals, have crashed to their deaths since 1955.

The man whose cars bring glory and death to so many is a mysterious figure—a recluse who never goes to races, who is rarely seen in public, who appears to suffer intensely each time a driver is killed, who protests that he loves his drivers like sons, but sends them out the next week anyway.

Enzo Ferrari, sixty-four years old, is a stern, unapproachable man. All who come in contact with him defer to him. No one sits down until he does. He has no intimates. He is addressed only as Commendatore, the rank to which he was raised by the Italian king before the war, in recognition of the glorious victories he had won for Italy.

Ferrari was born in Carpi, a village nine miles north of Modena, present capital of the Ferrari kingdom. He was a mule-shoer in the Italian army during World War I.

After the war he had a short, undistinguished career as a race driver, taking over in 1925 as team manager for Alfa Romeo. When the Alfas quit racing, Ferrari bought the cars and raced them under his own name. Most of the great drivers of that epoch worked for him: Nuvolari, Varzi, Campari, and others.

In 1939 Ferrari came to Modena to build his own cars. War began. Worried about possible bombings, Ferrari moved the factory to Maranello, ten miles west, and spent the war making machine tools.

The first Ferrari cars appeared after the war. It is said that the transition from tools to cars was made thanks to the devotion of workers who labored on the cars after hours. This is part of the legend which surrounds Ferrari, and may or may not be true. Today Ferrari's factory domain covers an area equivalent to two city blocks, and no one enters it without a pass.

Ferrari produces and sells about 600 luxury convertibles and coupes a year at prices ranging from $9,300 (if bought in lire at the factory) to nearly $15,000 (if delivered to a James Stewart or William Holden in Hollywood). At Christmas 1962 Ferrari claimed that every car he would build in 1963 had already been ordered.

To produce 600 cars a year Ferrari employs about 300 men. And to produce a dozen racers a year he employs forty more, which gives a fair idea of how the man thinks and what he really loves. Each racing car must cost Ferrari at least $40,000.

He is no philanthropist. He does not lose money. The cost of racing is met partly by starting and prize money, partly by a subsidy paid Ferrari by the Italian automobile industry and part of it can be written off as advertising for the luxury models.

THE FERRARI MARQUE has been the most successful that has ever raced, and it is the only one that has gone on and on in every type of racing, without stopping.

Other marques (Mercedes, Alfa Romeo, Maserati, and the rest) always withdrew from time to time for lack of manpower or money or because they had no real need to keep racing. Enzo Ferrari has always seen to it that the manpower and money were there. The need he has supplied from deep inside himself. The perfection of the racing automobile, the perfection of the breed, is what he lives for.

He is an autocratic man. Things must be done his way, or not at all. Harry Schell called him "an impossible man to work for." His designers and engineers never last more than a year or two. Team managers last no longer. They are not really team managers anyway; they are extensions of the telephone line from Modena.

The cars are true Ferrari cars. They mirror Ferrari, and no one else. Ferrari's engines are always more powerful than other marques can mount. Ferrari is not an engineer, but he knows engines. He has insights. He forces his ideas on his engineers and if one quits, he gets another. And his engines stay more powerful.

His cars are tougher, stronger, and break down far less. "My cars must be beautiful," says Ferrari. "But more than that, they must not stop out on the circuit. For then people will say, 'What a pity, it was so pretty.'" And his voice is tinged with disgust. Because Ferrari cars are stronger, they are also inherently safer. All drivers recognize this, and admire it, even if they cannot admire Ferrari personally.

Ferrari is an archconservative. He won't change anything until it gets defeated in race after race. His cars are bigger and heavier than the others, and he does not care. "They have more horsepower," Ferrari says stubbornly, "and they don't break down."

He never pays attention to what his drivers say. Their suggested improvements are ignored. He pretends to love them, but no one believes he really does, and many who have worked for him despise him.

The central fact of Enzo Ferrari's life is death. But not the death of drivers. It was the death in 1956 of his son, Alfredo, called Dino, of leukemia at the age of twenty-five. The boy had been bedridden part of every year from the age of sixteen. He kept asking his father why his body was so feeble. Ferrari had no answer. He had had much experience in death, but death had never been personal until now.

Ferrari had planned that the boy should be the greatest automotive engineer of all time, that his own name would be perpetuated by the greatness he had left behind in his son. This was his dream, all bound up in the son he worshipped and knew was going to die.

Ferrari has not accustomed himself to Dino's death. He keeps Dino's memory alive in every possible way, even ordering the boy's name embossed on the engine blocks of the race cars. Every day he is in Modena, Ferrari visits Dino's tomb, locks himself inside and broods. Associates say he goes there when drivers are killed too.

Ferrari's life has become his cars. He works twelve to fifteen hours a day, Sundays included. "A man has no need of entertainment," he told me. "Entertainment only distracts from his duty. If a man has his duty, that is enough."

Ferrari is said to be wealthy, but all the money goes back into his cars. He lives with his wife and three dogs in a five-room apartment over the warehouse in Modena, and when he goes to the factory in Maranello he drives a Fiat. His two offices are starkly furnished. The only ornament in Maranello is a big black-bordered picture of Dino with votive lights burning under it. In Modena there is a similar funereal picture of Dino and, standing in a row on a shelf, photos of his six contract drivers for the year. The snapshots and the men are impermanent. Any errant breeze, any minute error of judgment at 150 miles per hour, could blow one over.

FERRARI WILL NOT negotiate with drivers. They take what he offers, or they leave—and the pay is less than elsewhere. At the end of one season, Phil Hill and Dan Gurney asked for raises. Ferrari fired Gurney. Wanting to keep Hill, he announced that Hill was retiring from the sport, and would not drive a Ferrari in the U.S. Grand Prix the next month. Hill did in fact drive in that race. "Ferrari decided to give me one last chance," Hill said glumly. "And I took it." He did not get the raise.

Ferrari makes little effort to sign the best drivers each year. The best drivers sign with

factories which offer the best terms; with Ferrari there is no question of terms. Ferrari's drivers usually have a flaw, and usually it is the same flaw: a need to drive faster than is, for them, safe. Ferrari's drivers are usually men who crash a great deal: Musso, Portago, Castellotti, Trips, Behra, Rodriguez. And currently, Willy Mairesse. Such men are nervous, inaccurate, non-prudent men. They drive very fast; they have tremendous desire to excel. Never mind the peril.

They appeal to something in Ferrari.

Ferrari also hired Tony Brooks—for a year. And he kept Phil Hill and Olivier Gendebien for many years, always, it seemed, against his better judgment.

The primary reason Ferraris have crashed more than other marques is that so many Ferrari drivers have had this temperamental flaw. The secondary reason is that Ferrari would always hire six drivers for three cars—the regulars had to push to the limit to stay ahead of the reserves. Nor would Ferrari name a team leader as other marques did. He left the drivers to settle for themselves upon a team leader. If this meant a dogfight for first place during a race, Ferrari would watch from Modena with an amused glint in his eye. In 1961 Hill and Trips were virtually tied for the world championship. The Ferrari cars were so strong that one or the other had to win each race—nothing else could challenge. Both drivers wanted Ferrari to name a team leader; it is dangerous to race it out in identical cars. But Ferrari never said a word.

Finally in the next to last race, the Italian Grand Prix, Trips stalled at the start. Hill got off to a big lead. As Trips hurried to catch up, he must have thought: this is the break that will settle the world championship, a bad break for me; I must hold my foot down, hold my foot down.

If Ferrari had named a team leader one way or the other, Trips would not have driven those first two frantic laps in such a heavy-footed panic. They were the last laps of his life.

The next year Hill hardly even tried. The Ferrari was again somewhat slower than other cars, but probably not as slow as Hill made it look. At the factory in Maranello, men watched Ferrari and then publicly expressed Ferrari's thoughts. Hill has lost his enthusiasm, they said.

Hill said: "They think I should go out there in an inferior car and sacrifice myself to the honor and glory of Ferrari. There have been too many sacrifices already. I won't be another. I won't be one of their sacrifices."

The Cooper Car Co. Ltd.

THE COOPER FACTORY is as bright and shiny as a suburban gas station. There are no guards, no gates. On a warm, sunny afternoon, English school children stroll by without a glance. The portentous gloom of the Ferrari assembly line is unknown here.

Down through the years the sale of showroom models has been the principal aim of most factories producing race cars; if a factory forgot this, it failed. Usually it failed anyway, or started to. The production of race cars is overpoweringly expensive. Mercedes, Maserati, Aston Martin, Jaguar, Auto Union, and many other automotive giants were driven to the wall by their racing programs. Some lesser factories went out of business without a ripple.

But the Cooper Car Co. of Surbiton, England, which builds no showroom models at all, not only survives, it even thrives on producing and selling racing cars only—sixty-six of them in 1962. This had never been done before; it may never be done again. Charles and John Cooper are skillful, and they are also very, very lucky. They came to the surface in a society which wanted race cars, plenty of race cars, plenty of cheap race cars; and they stumbled on a curious, untried philosophy: racing for the common man.

In 1962, working in the back of the garage shown here, and a nearby machine shop, employing only forty people including secretaries at peak season, the Coopers built three Grand Prix team cars; twelve Grand Prix cars (last year's model); forty-five Formula Junior cars, and six racing sports cars.

The three team cars were not for sale. Had they been, they would have cost about $25,000. Two were raced by Bruce McLaren and Tony Maggs, the contract drivers, and the third was a spare. The twelve versions of last year's model were sold to enthusiasts for about $14,000 each. The Formula Junior car cost $4,500, and the six racing sports cars were sold for $15,700 each. One of the reasons Coopers are so cheap is that there are no dealerships anywhere in the world. If you want to buy a Cooper you write to Surbiton. The average waiting period is four months, but if you crash a Cooper on a Sunday, the factory will repair it for you in time to race the following Sunday—provided you still want to.

At that, Coopers are much more expensive than they used to be. In 1959, the year Jack Brabham drove a team Cooper to the world championship, a similar car was sold to Stirling Moss for $12,600. This is surely the cheapest winning Grand Prix car ever built.

The Cooper factory started as a gas station in 1920. It still looks like a gas station from outside, and plenty of gas is yet sold. Nominally the boss is Charles Cooper, who is sixty-nine years old and not in the best of health. John Cooper, thirty-nine, runs things now. He is a friendly, enthusiastic man, married and with children. He loves cars of all kinds, not just racers. He loves going to all the races where he serves as pit manager and, when he gets excited enough, as signal man too (see photo page 181). John Cooper has no hero worship for his drivers; they are his pals. They help him put the cars together (no Ferrari driver is allowed to touch the machines) and afterwards all go out for a few beers. Successful as he has been, John Cooper has taken on no airs. He is not aloof. He is proud of this. In his selection of drivers, Cooper will have nothing to do with wild young men, nor with those possessed by some demon for speed. Cooper hired Masten Gregory, a crasher, but dropped him

as soon as possible. Cooper's drivers, Brabham, McLaren, are steady, hard-working types. They love the machinery as Cooper himself does. They drive as fast as they can in a quiet, controlled way. They very rarely crash. Cooper has not lost a team driver yet.

THE COOPER factory came into being in 1946 when young John decided he wanted to race. He and his father and some mechanics slapped together a tiny 500-cc car in five weeks. It weighed only 550 pounds, and was powered by a motorcycle engine.

There were many races in England for tiny cars at that time. The Cooper was dependable, consistent, and, most of all, cheap. Enthusiasts began to ask Charles Cooper to make them a car too. So the next year, 1947, twelve cars were built. In 1948, a nineteen-year-old boy named Stirling Moss bought a Cooper and won eleven of his first fifteen races. Orders for more of the tiny race cars poured in so fast the Coopers couldn't handle them all. In the years that followed, the Coopers built bigger and bigger cars fitted with bigger and bigger engines. But it was not until 1959 the production of the original 500-cc cars finally was stopped.

In 1955, Coventry-Climax, primarily makers of fire pump engines, supplied the Coopers with a racing engine for the first time. This was the best engine available in England, but was still too small to match Italian and German machines. The Coopers struggled along with the undersized engine until 1958 when some magical driving by Moss won the Argentine Grand Prix with it. Now Coventry-Climax got enthusiastic, beefed up the little engine to normal size, and Coopers dominated Grand Prix racing in 1959 and 1960, Brabham winning the world championship both years.

All factories buy brakes, carburetors, tires, clutches, et al., from plants making these goods. The Coopers (together with Lotus, Lola, and Brabham among current marques) also buy engines ready made from Coventry-Climax. The Coopers manufacture everything else. Trial and error figure largely in putting together the cars, and the test drivers—first Brabham, now McLaren—contribute a lot.

The Coopers' strength is road holding. John Cooper says that the 1961 Ferrari's suspension was an exact copy of the 1960 Cooper. This delighted him. "If something is beating you," he said, "you must either think up something better or copy it. No good blundering about."

Lately the Coopers have given their name and advice to the huge British Motor Corporation which manufactures something called the Mini-Cooper. John Cooper enters a team of Mini-Coopers in races, and has five drivers under contract. A Mini-Cooper tuned for racing costs only about $2,500.

"Think of it, you can be a race driver for $2,500. Racing that cheap has never been possible before." John Cooper is very proud as he talks, for he knows this is his doing, and no one else's.

As for the team Grand Prix cars, it takes months to build them, and John Cooper lives in dread that in an early race one season his drivers might manage to wreck all three. If this happened there would be no more Coopers that season, unless Cooper decided for form's sake to enter some older models lying around the garage. Cooper, whose racing department is only six or eight people, simply cannot build his team cars in a hurry. Ferrari could and has. Four Ferraris were wrecked during the 1957 Grand Prix de Monaco, for instance; four new ones raced in the next Grand Prix event on the program.

Ferrari has the men and means to rebuild team cars almost instantly. Often he has done so. Cooper could not match this. Of course, he has never had to—which is another of the major differences between Ferrari Automobili and the Cooper Car Co. Ltd.

Part Four:
Practice

The Paddock

USUALLY each marque rents garage space in the town nearest the circuit. The cars are brought out by van in the early morning and unloaded, then are worked on again. Mechanics are never satisfied, never leave the cars alone.

Earplugs

AS MECHANICS drive the cars from the paddock in back to the pits in front, the cars are slow-moving, but their engines roar, the noise gathering, getting close. Such noise as this has weight. The very air seems heavy—and getting heavier. About to go to work, drivers put their earplugs in; to sit head pressed against such noise would leave a man partially deaf for hours, if not for life. Some drivers use drugstore earplugs, some use cotton. Most use wax. They begin to knead the wax as the cars come out from the paddock. The ball of wax has been lying soiled, well used, in their pockets, but under their fingers it softens, and then they force it carefully into their ears.

Helmets

EACH DRIVER has carefully polished his goggles—or visor if it is raining—although sometimes the wives do this. The driver withdraws his helmet from the bulky satchel all drivers carry and which, on a train or plane, could identify one as easily as a doctor is marked by the shape of his bag. Until the war, drivers wore linen aviator's helmets.

Then they wore fiber ones which looked glamorous, but gave little protection. Now most wear helmets close to those of a jet pilot: expensive, solid, tight-fitting. Lastly the driver pulls on his gloves. They are light, tight, and the leather palms stick to the steering wheel better than skin does. The driver is ready.

The First Day

MOST CIRCUITS are big enough so that drivers, at the start of practice, dispatch themselves anytime after the circuit has been cleared and the practice session officially opened. But at Monte Carlo, 1.9 miles around, Race Director Louis Chiron, a former racing champion, dispatches the cars one by one, a few seconds apart, so that they do not hurtle into the narrow streets, the sharp corners *en masse*. The Monaco circuit is so tiny that multiple collisions in the race are common. But in practice Chiron can minimize the risk by the careful spacing of cars at the start.

Reconnaissance at Speed

THE FIRST LAPS are for reconnaissance. At each circuit the road changes slightly from year to year. After the first, relatively slow laps, the driver will, if he is satisfied with his machine, try for a fast-timed lap. Positions on the starting grid are assigned according to fastest practice laps. Usually the best laps are done on the last day of practice, the driver having found, finally, the best line through turns, best tires, best gear ratios. But even the first day, when a slower driver is in the way, there is frantic signaling, trying to attract the slower man's attention to his mirror. All drivers are supposed to watch their mirrors, but some hardly ever do.

Loved Ones

MEANWHILE, back at the pits, the wives, sisters, girlfriends are in position for what must be, to them, a long afternoon. Some are already polishing their nails or talking about jewelry. It is easy to tell, looking at a row of them, whose driver is out on the track and even, approximately, how soon he is due around.

The Casino

THE CIRCUIT MAY wind through meadows or forests or a town, past grazing cows that don't look up, or geese that don't look up either, or the world's most famous casino. Race cars take casino turn (above) at 60 miles per hour—normal speed limit is 16 miles per hour. More than one car has piled into the casino wall—called in the trade: "trying to enter the casino without paying."

Noise

AT THE PITS there is constant commotion—and colossal noise. Drivers coming in to complain about their cars must shout over their own engine noise and that of other engines being revved up and down nearby. Mechanics shout (right), engineers shout, wives shout. Everybody shouts. Engine fumes rise all about. The fumes are sweet, sharp, the distinctive odor of motor racing. But mostly the pit area, during practice, is ear-splitting noise.

94

The Wait

THE PRACTICE may last three hours, but in all that time the driver is busy perhaps thirty minutes. He does his laps in small bunches. In between, the cars are rolled away. Things are done to them. The drivers wait. A few have brought books to the pits; using helmets as pillows, they would lie on the pit counter and read. But reading is hard to do amid so much noise and movement. Most drivers, like Ricardo Rodriguez, left, just sit there, staring, sometimes alone, sometimes with their wives, until the car comes back again and (next page) they go out onto the circuit once more.

Fight for Seconds

THE DRIVER is a nervous man. After waiting impatiently for mechanics to be done, he hurries through the forest, along the harbor front, trying to cut fractional seconds off his lap time. By the time practice ends there is a layer of rubber on the corners. You can read the best line through each corner by wherever the street is blackest.

Last Laps

FOR THE DRIVER nothing exists except himself, his car, and the circuit. For each fractional second eliminated he moves one notch higher on the starting grid. Soon it is late afternoon of the last day, the sun is low, and hardly anybody is still watching the cars go round. The cars circulating now are the very poorest and the very fastest; the middle positions on the grid were secured long ago, and if you were tenth best it is not worth wearing the car out trying to qualify ninth or eighth. But if you did not qualify at all, you are still out there trying. And if you qualified second or third, there is still a chance, in the last few minutes before practice ends, that you can win the pole position. Usually the pole position is worth no more, in the race itself, than any other position in the front row. But it is worth a lot psychologically, and also financially. There are always prizes for fastest practice lap, either money or silverware or, at Reims, one hundred bottles of champagne.

Practice Ends

NO DRIVER is happy. Each feels the machine was not right and that tomorrow he will be left behind. Mechanics and engineers swarm about the car, checking temperature gauges and rev counters. The technician from Dunlop Tires measures wear and temperature of the rubber. The driver stares straight ahead, or glances disgustedly up at his crew. He removes his steering wheel preparatory to climbing out, hugs it to his chest, and sits there, worried about tomorrow, fearing the worst. The stands are empty. The pit area empties out. The unhappy driver rubs his eyes, body sagging dispiritedly. He has qualified fourth. If mechanics cannot do something tonight, he will have no chance, no chance at all, tomorrow.

The Long Night

IN A DIMLY lit garage, a mechanic scans the driver's plea for changes to be effected by morning. The mechanics will work all night. Most racing mechanics would earn more money and see more of their families if they chose to repair expensive sedans somewhere. They would certainly get more sleep. Of course, there is no excitement to sedans. Racing mechanics rarely give it up. The faces are the same year after year.

The Day of the Race

Morning

FEW DRIVERS can sleep. Most are up early, bathed, shaved, combed, restless. They may stand on a balcony with nothing to say to each other. When a visitor comes by, one clowns, one stares into the distance.

Later they dine, though without much appetite. Members of a team usually lunch together. Probably it is not noon, yet. Though the race does not start till three or later, they must leave for the circuit before the traffic jam builds up around it.

Phil Hill (far left) and Graham Hill (below) won the Belgian and Dutch Grand Prixs the days these pictures were taken.

Noon

SOME DRIVERS wish to be alone. For them the race has weight, and the morning passes slowly. But soon it becomes time to go out to the circuit. Though it is still early, mobs of kids (and a few adults) wait impatiently for each driver to arrive. When he does, books, pictures, programs are proffered to be signed. Most drivers sign a few. The drivers are nervous and lose patience quickly.

One Hour to Go

THE CARS WAIT in row in the paddock, with plastic over carburetors to keep out dirt. Mechanics give finishing touches, while people who have bought paddock passes (available on some circuits) wander about. At booths nearby, enthusiasts buy, or consider buying, accessories such as Stirling Moss steering wheels—guaranteed to increase highway speed by 10 miles per hour or more.

Warming Up Engines

AN ENGINE STARTS UP, becomes a high-pitched, penetrating scream. A little girl covers her ears. One by one other engines burst into applause. They seem to set each other off, the way one lion in a zoo starts a roar along the cages. A driver, here Jack Brabham, revs his engine up and down, up and down. The noise is stupendous.

The Press

IN ITS VARIOUS DISGUISES the press prowls about, observing, filming, interviewing. Scores of men, always the same ones, come to every race. A few report for newspapers. Most represent the motor racing trade publications of the world and can discourse learnedly on revs, gearboxes, and the like. They know the most esoteric details of all the cars, and they pass this mass of information on to their readers who, presumably, consume it. The motor racing press is much less interested in the personalities of the drivers, and is not interested in drivers' private lives at all. I do not know why so many of these "motoring journalists" sport beards or Sherlock Holmes hats or wear their hair a bit long. Despite hirsute adornments, most of these men are accepted and respected by the drivers. They know cars, and on the whole, they are more accurate in the information they supply than many journalists in other fields.

Twenty Minutes to Go

IF IT IS RAINING HARD, or if a preliminary race has left oil on the road, there will be a single reconnaissance lap before the race. Usually there is none. The cars are driven or pushed from the paddock out to the front of the pits. There, engines are revved up and down until certain engine temperatures are attained. Then mechanics wheel the machines up to the starting line, and the drivers straggle up behind. It is now about twenty minutes before the race will start. On the line the cars are kept covered from rain or sun. Drivers and crowd wait out the final minutes before the start.

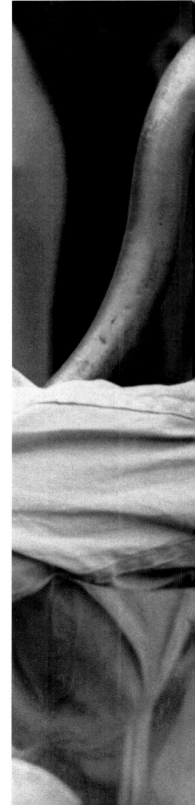

124

Waiting

THE FINAL MINUTES are the longest and worst. The waiting gets on everybody's nerves. The drivers have been waiting all day, but it has not seemed interminable until now. A driver waits beside his pregnant wife; she talks across a fence to friends, but he stares at the ground not listening. Nearby, another driver waits in his machine, eyes tightly closed, alone with private thoughts, alone with what he soon must do.

Tension

THE WAITING goes on and on, and soon everybody is yawning nervously. Bruce McLaren yawns. Willy Mairesse yawns. The wife of Jo Bonnier yawns.

The Kiss

ABRUPTLY, it is time. A driver embraces his wife. Though she clings to him the embrace lasts only a moment. Then she is left behind. He, standing beside his peers, listens to last-minute instructions from the starter. From the left: Innes Ireland, Alan Stacey, Tony Brooks, Stirling Moss, Bruce McLaren, Phil Hill, Richie Ginther (squatting), Wolfgang von Trips, Dan Gurney (partially hidden), Joakim Bonnier, and Roy Salvadori.

Part Six:

The Race

One Second to Go

WITH ONE HAND on the wheel, perhaps without taking his eyes off the temperature gauges, the driver has signaled that he is ready. Now, an instant before the flag falls, his attention is riveted so fiercely on the upheld flag that he can scarcely breathe. The car is in gear, foot holding the clutch to the floor, engine revving up and down. The driver's mouth hangs open. He is absolutely, breathlessly taut.

When the flag drops he lurches forward in his seat as if to push the car forward with the movement of his body. His right foot on the accelerator goes down to the floor. His left foot lifts swiftly and the car spurts forward. The noise of twenty accelerating Grand Prix machines is deafening. The smoke rises behind them. They are gone.

The Grid

THE GRID at Silverstone in the rain: the flag has just dropped. Stirling Moss, car No. 4, has already let in his clutch, inducing slight wheelspin, causing the halo of water around his right rear tire. None of the other front row drivers, McLaren, Brabham, and Graham Hill, has reacted, yet. Moss, who got the quickest start, went on to win this race by more than a lap.

Perfect Start

IF THE START is perfect, the cars will reach the first corner still tightly bunched, as here. They will cross the trolley tracks and start up the long, straight street still virtually nose to tail. This start, behind the beach at Oporto, Portugal, was a fine one. No driver got left at the post, there were no shunts or collisions. The only thing disorderly is the crowd. There are too many people standing about in the street, particularly the man in uniform (right side of photo), who has just stepped off the curb. If two cars were to touch during the wild scramble round this corner, one could easily be batted into him.

Not So Perfect Start

NOT ALL STARTS are perfect. Here are two which went less well. Left is a bone-jarring triple collision caused when starter Toto Roche (the fat man on page 130) signaled the start of the Grand Prix de France at Reims by waving his flag sideways (instead of up and down), while the drivers were still watching the "Thirty Seconds to Go" sign. Some cars started on this signal, and some rammed cars ahead which did not start fast enough.

And below, Innes Ireland flings up a frantic hand to warn cars behind that he has stalled on the line. Unable to engage first gear, he could not start as fast as the others. To minimize risk of accident, he chose to let other cars rush by in a blur, before attempting to start at all.

Downhill

OCCASIONALLY, THE START is at the brow of a hill, so that the massed cars, racing away from the starting line, seem to hesitate, then plunge into some harrowing void. To watch the cars speed into that first corner is no less harrowing, no less wonderful. This is what road racing is all about: the race cars are speeding down hills, rounding acute, reverse camber corners at speeds normal men would not dare on a wide, straight highway. The skill and control which goes into this is incredible, thrilling, and fills the spectator with wonder. Wonder is one of the chief emotions motor racing gives. The drivers maintain a control of their machines which is absolute. And yet at the last moment a photographer (below) cowers behind a pole, unable to believe that such speed, such dust and noise, can really be controlled at all.

The Empty Track

THE CARS HAVE disappeared. The noise diminishes into the forest or behind the buildings of the town. It may be two minutes or five or ten, depending on the size of the circuit, before the cars are back. In the meantime the road in front of the pits is soundless. Across in the grandstand people stir, light cigarettes. There is nothing to do but wait. An owner waits, a driver's wife waits, in the aching suspense of the first lap. Who got off in which position? There had been too much noise, dust, and smoke

to be sure. What is happening off across the circuit?

Now the noise swells. In a moment the mass of cars will burst by again, perhaps all of them, perhaps missing one or two. The owner, Colin Chapman of Lotus, will know better what his chances are. The wife, Betty Hill, will see Graham Hill in first or fifth or tenth place and be reassured. Whatever the verdict of the first lap, everyone will relax. It is better to know the worst, than to sit there fearing it.

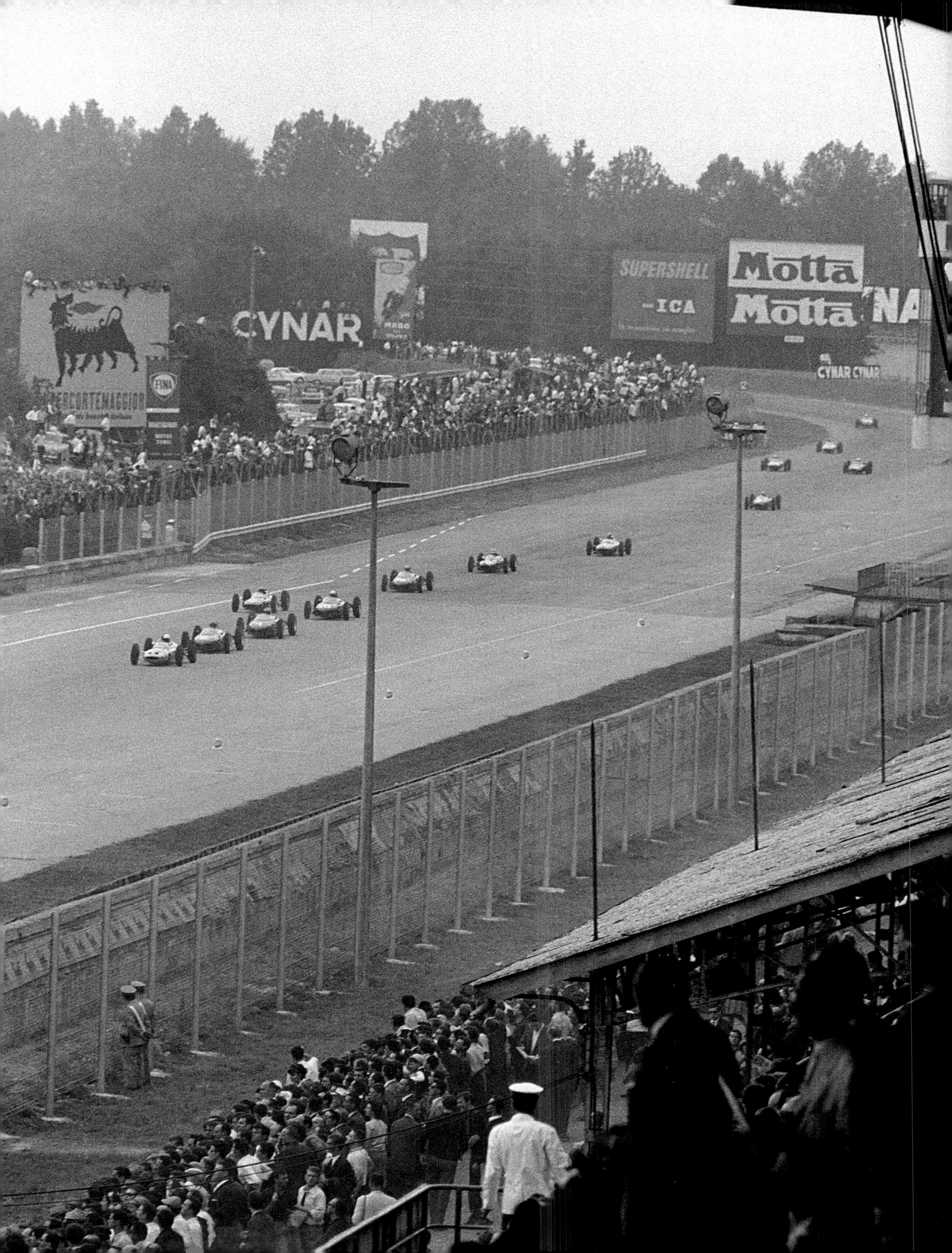
CYNAR
SUPERSHELL
ICA
Motta
Motta
CYNAR CYNAR

The Circuits

NOW THE TENSION diminishes for a time. The different circuits may favor different drivers, and they almost always favor one car or another. The race will last between two and three hours, and now in the early laps the circuit must be allowed to take its toll.

At Reims a car which can't be kept on the boil will soon break down, for the Thillois straight (right) is the longest and fastest in Grand Prix racing. The 1960 machines shown here were clocked at over 175 miles per hour, the current smaller cars at about 160. Such speeds are not attained anywhere else. The Thillois straight is about two miles long, part of it downhill through wheat fields that are golden brown in the July sun. The Reims circuit itself is 5.6 miles around, is roughly triangular in shape, and the average winning speeds there are about 125 miles per hour.

But at Zandvoort, Holland (below), the winner will average only about 95. The circuit, 2.6 miles around, winds in and out and around grass-covered sand dunes behind the North Sea beach. It is road-holding that counts at Zandvoort; the car that is hard to handle will soon drop back.

Aintree—
The Nürburgring

THE CIRCUIT at Aintree, England, is roughly triangular in shape and most of the way round it runs beside the grass horse racing track and the high impenetrable hedges of the Grand National Steeplechase. One lap equals three miles and the average speed for Grand Prix cars is about 91 miles per hour. Aintree, being as flat and dull as Britain's ex-airport circuits (Goodwood, Silverstone), favors road-holding over brute speed. These courses have nothing to do with road racing, but in England there is no alternative. The law forbids closing off public roads or streets (as at Reims, Monaco, etc.) and no major private circuits exist as at Zandvoort or the Nürburgring.

The Nürburgring, right, the longest circuit, runs through the Eifel Mountains of West Germany, for 14.2 miles, about 175 curves per lap. Its average speed is 95 miles per hour. It is the most difficult road racing circuit in the world, the most dangerous and the best loved by drivers. It does not favor any car; it favors the best driver. A virtuoso, like Stirling Moss, can win here over cars 20 miles per hour faster than his own. The Nürburgring is one of the most exciting places to see a race, if you walk through the forest from corner to corner, and the British circuits presently in use are the dullest, no matter where you watch from.

Portugal

THESE ARE THE TWO Portuguese circuits, both of which are beautiful, dramatic, exciting, and true tests of driver skill and car stamina. The Portuguese Grand Prix existed from 1950 to 1960, the Lisbon and Oporto circuits alternating as site, but now has lapsed, apparently for lack of money, perhaps only temporarily. The crowds at Lisbon were fairly small, but at Oporto (right) they were enormous.

Both circuits were public streets closed off for the day, connected to a street through a wooded public park. One was in the suburbs on a hill above Lisbon (above). The other wound inland from the street fronting on the harbor and beach at Oporto.

To go all the way to Portugal was difficult, especially for mechanics driving the vans, and there were other problems too. But the circuits were admirable, the settings dramatic, and everybody wishes the Grand Prix of Portugal would resume.

Above, Moss wins the 1959 Grand Prix at Lisbon at an average speed of 95.32 miles per hour, the lap there being 3.38 miles around. At Oporto the next year, Moss, in Lotus No. 12, finished only fifth, then was disqualified for a rules infraction. The Oporto circuit, 4.6 miles per lap, was lapped at 109 miles per hour.

Monte Carlo

THE STREET CLIMBS to the Hotel de Paris, crosses in front of the casino, then plunges to the harbor again—where people watch from yachts. The lap is 1.9 miles, and the race average only 70 miles per hour, slowest of all Grand Prixs.

Breakdown

THE CIRCUIT EXACTS its toll. Cars break down and are rolled away. A driver signs his "retirement advice" for race officials. For him the race is over. A driver, stalled in the forest, rides in atop the sputtering machine of a colleague. Jack Brabham, whose Brabham has failed in its first outing, is grim, unhappy, worried.

The Spin

THE MOST COMMON loss of control is the spin. The driver enters the turn a mite too fast. It may only be one mile per hour too fast, but it is enough. The tire marks show the path which No. 15 has taken. The back of the car breaks adhesion, and the rear tires slide out sideways, until the car is broadside in the road. If the car is going fast enough it may spin completely around two or more times, shoot off the road, and crash into something. But this turn here at Zandvoort is very tight, the cars making only about 40 miles per hour. No. 15, driven by the Dutch amateur, Ben Pon, has apparently spun only once. By the time the car was broadside in the road, the sideways forces and the forward forces were about equal. The back wheels slid forward straight across the axis of the curve, with the front part of the car pirouetting around them. The back wheels, with the weight on them and sliding at the peak of forward speed combined with outthrusting centrifugal force, have left black welts on the road; the trace of the pirouetting front wheels is dimmer.

Spins happen to everyone, the good drivers and the bad—although rather more often to the bad. Pon got into two of them

in this particular race, his first world championship Grand Prix, and his second spin ended with the car on top of him in a ditch.

Spins are very spectacular to watch. But they usually happen in slow turns where the driver can take a chance on exceeding the absolute limit—he would be a fool to take such a chance when the speeds are very high. Thus people rarely get hurt in spins. The car spins to a stop usually without even leaving the road. Of course all that sideways strain could crack suspension or steering, and no one gets into spins for a joke. But drivers in a hurry in slow turns do sometimes risk spins, accelerating until the road feels like glass under their wheels, hoping to save fractional seconds, hoping that the back end won't go out from under them. In a passenger car spins are very dangerous because the cars are top-heavy and they can easily turn over. Racing cars are very low, very difficult to flip, and most drivers in a spin are not only not scared, they are probably cursing.

The biggest danger in spins is that the car or cars behind you are so close they will plow into you when you are broadside in the road. Ben Pon, here, was lucky. All the trailing cars got by him safely.

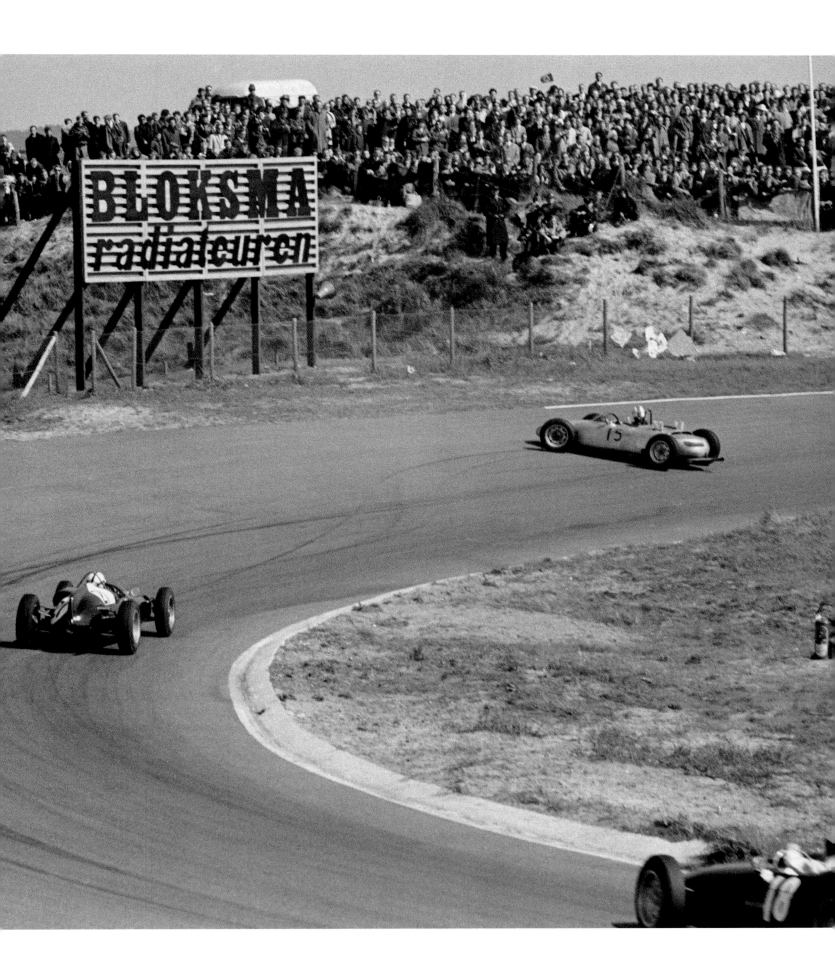

The Spin (2)

BUT IN THIS SPIN, luck was not there for everybody. Willy Mairesse, entering a left-hand, ninety-degree corner too fast, has spun about halfway through the corner or a bit more, so that his car comes to a stop blocking the exit from the corner, broadside in the road and concealed from the cars coming up behind it. Drivers behind Mairesse, entering this turn about 40 miles per hour, cannot see Mairesse stalled broadside in the road until they are half through the turn, and by then it is too late to do much about it. Jo Bonnier (left) has chosen to go outside Mairesse, and he gets by. But the next car into the turn is the Lotus of Trevor Taylor. By now, only a second or two after the spin, Mairesse has restarted his engine and come partway around. Taylor has only an instant to decide which way to go. Opting to pass Mairesse on the inside, Taylor attempts to get past half in the rain gutter. He doesn't quite make it. The Lotus sends up a shower of water and stones as it strikes the Ferrari.

Clearing the Road

THE ACCIDENT is over and, for Taylor, so is the race. He is furious as he stands there, shouting back at Mairesse. The impact of the crash has straightened the Ferrari out. Mairesse stirs the gear lever, shoves it into first and speeds off. Eventually he won this race, the 1962 Grand Prix of Brussels. As for Taylor, he must now get the Lotus off its knee and off the road. A flag marshal, some spectators, and a cop come into the road to help. They are all worried about being hit by another car coming out of the same turn, and the cop has his whistle clenched in his teeth, although what good the whistle might do is difficult to say.

Motor racing is full of minor collisions. Once they are over, the only important thing is to clear the road, before more cars pile in. At Monte Carlo (next page) the road has been most competently cleared.

The Shunt

A SHUNT IS less serious (and more common) than a collision, because in a shunt all cars continue in the race; they just don't look as handsome as they used to. Taylor (top, opposite page) has got too close to a preceding car, probably in a slow turn, and its rear wheels or tailpipe or both have yanked off the nose of his cowling. The mouth of the Ferrari (bottom, opposite page) has been twisted into a snarl by a shunt; its angry driver, Count von Trips, is snarling too. Hardly any race is concluded without a shunt of some kind, or without a driver like Innes Ireland (below) peering incredulously back over his shoulder to see what has happened.

The Strain

LATE IN THE RACE there may be only half a dozen cars still running, tired drivers concentrating fiercely against the errors which have eliminated the others. Gurney and Ginther look flogged by wind, worn out. The face of Surtees (left,) is taut. Only Moss (bottom, opposite page) looks relaxed, imperturbable. Moss was not only the fastest driver, but the strongest too. All others slowed as they got tired. Moss never got tired, never slowed. The pressure Moss applied was unrelenting.

hell que j aime

Moments to Go

LEAD CAR BLURS past the harbor at Monte Carlo, opposite where frogmen wait to go down after any driver plunging through the barrier into the water; this has happened only once in the three decades of the race. Below: Baghetti and Bonnier race head-to-head past Reims pits few laps before end.

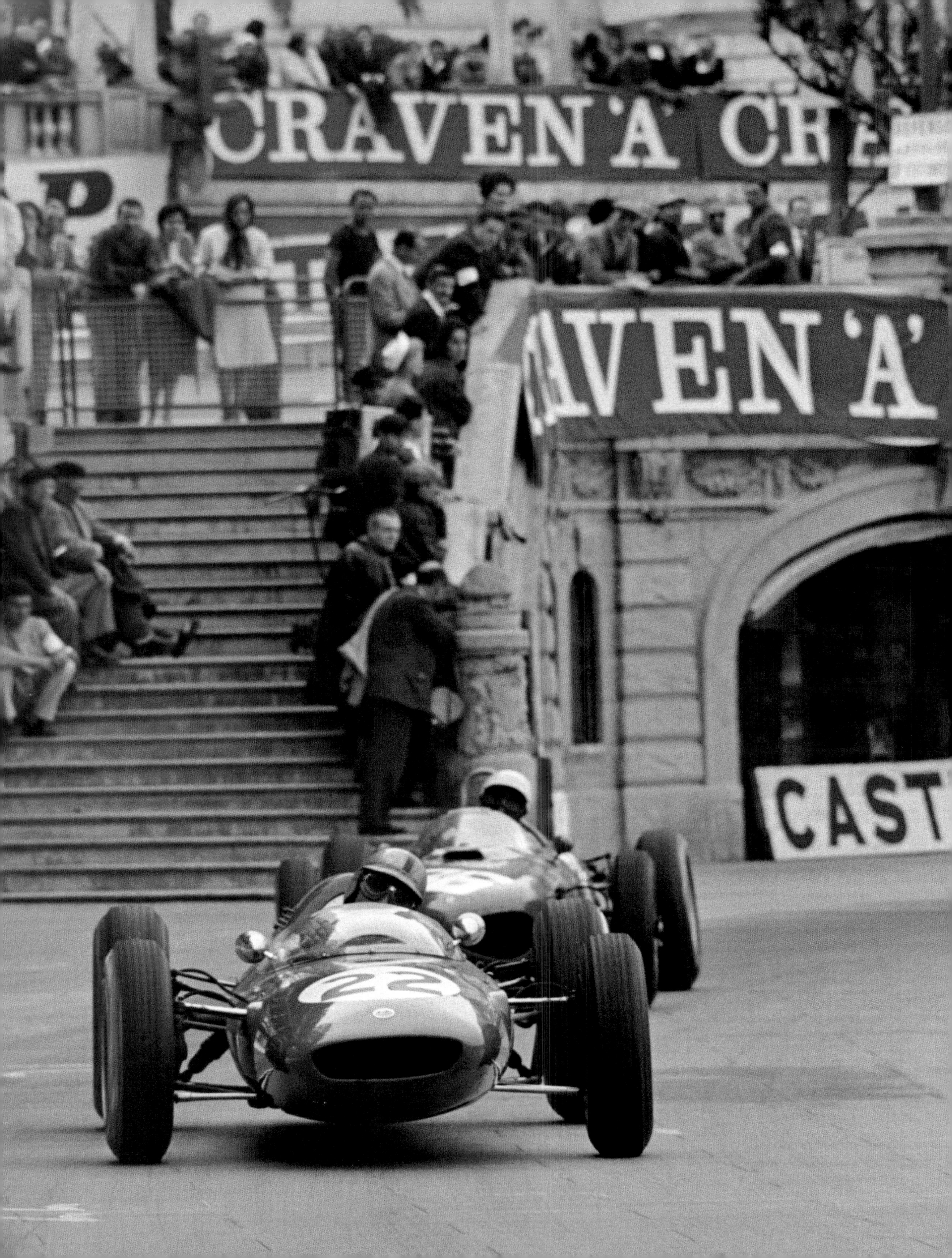
CRAVEN 'A' CRA
CRAVEN 'A'
CAST
22

Danger's Wife

AS FRANTIC pit signs show, the race has only a lap or two to go. Tired drivers have increased tempo to the breaking point. A wife watches in anguish. "Look at me," Betty Brabham said, the day this picture was taken, "my hair's a mess, I'm badly dressed, I'm a nervous wreck. What I need is a four-month vacation. Four months of not having to worry about Jack's life." That day Brabham clinched his second straight world championship.

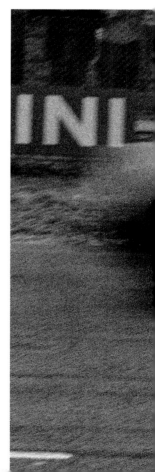

184

The Finish

AFTER BETWEEN TWO and three hundred miles, between two and three hours of hot, hard work, the finish line is crossed. The driver is making maximum speed. He flings up a hand in triumph. Mechanics, journalists, wives, fans stand on pit counters applauding. The race is over. He may have won by ten feet or ten miles; he does not care. The race is over. Now he will make a slow, joyous lap of the circuit, feeling safe and happy, waving at the crowd, dreaming of a hot bath, hoping that at the presentation ceremony, which now is imminent, no one will expect him to make a speech.

Triumph

IN FRONT OF the pits again, he slows to a stop. People run up to congratulate him, pat him, touch him. They surround the car. He stands up in his seat, grimy, sweaty, and then someone throws a wreath over his head. A police line is hurriedly formed to keep the onrushing crowd off him for a moment or two. Begging mechanics for water, the parched, grinning driver will guzzle two bottles or more. Then, boxed in by police, he will be hurried through the mob to the presentation stand. He will shake hands with celebrities. He will stand at attention as his country's flag is run up and its anthem played just for him. Flowers and trophies will be pressed upon him. He is hero to all the world. The winning drivers here and on the next four pages: McLaren, von Trips, Clark, Hill, and Moss with Prince Rainier and Princess Grace of Monaco.

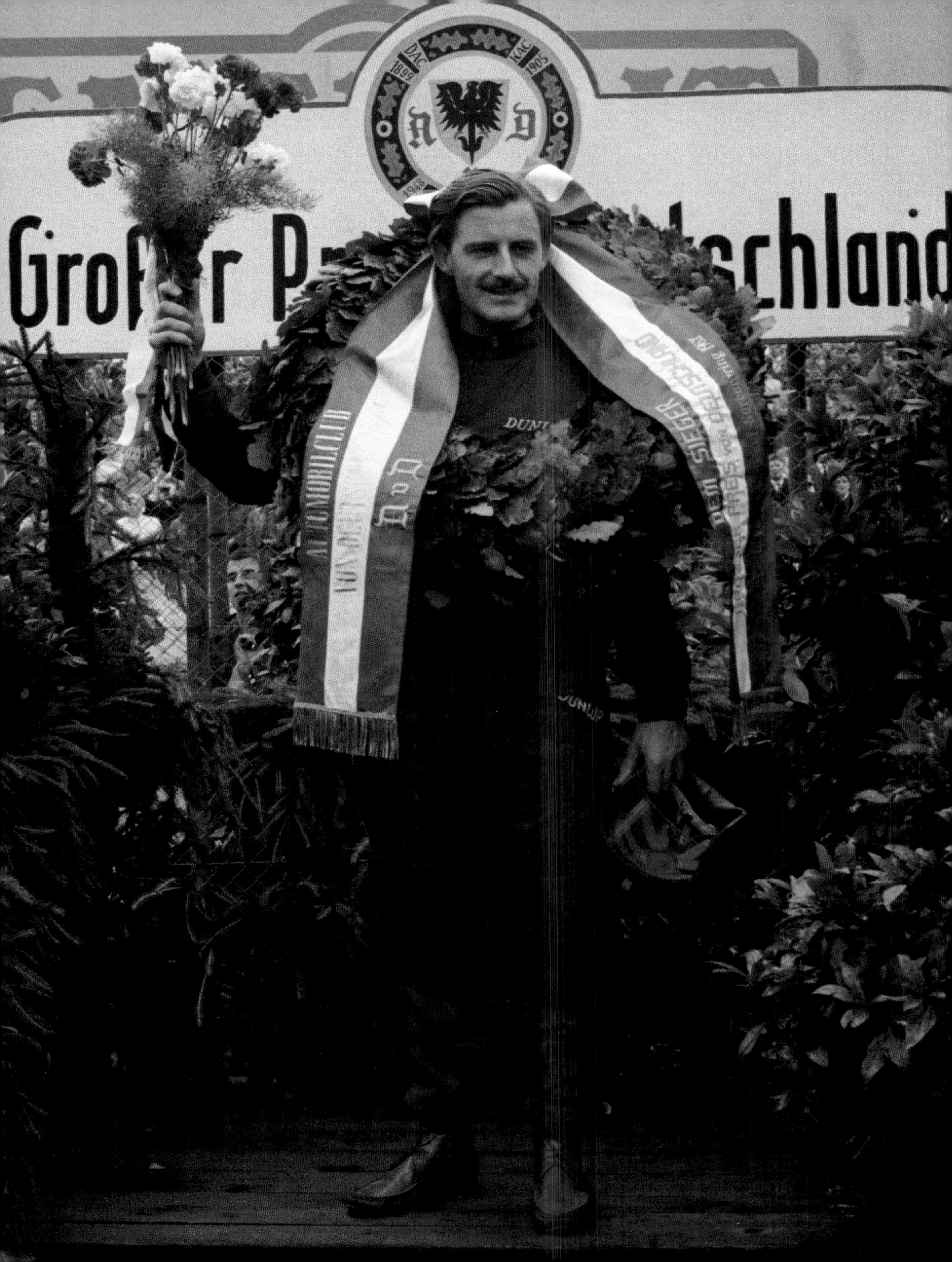
DAC
1899
KAC
1905
1948
AUTOMOBILCLUB
DEM SIEGER
DUNLOP

Part Seven:

The Price: Accident

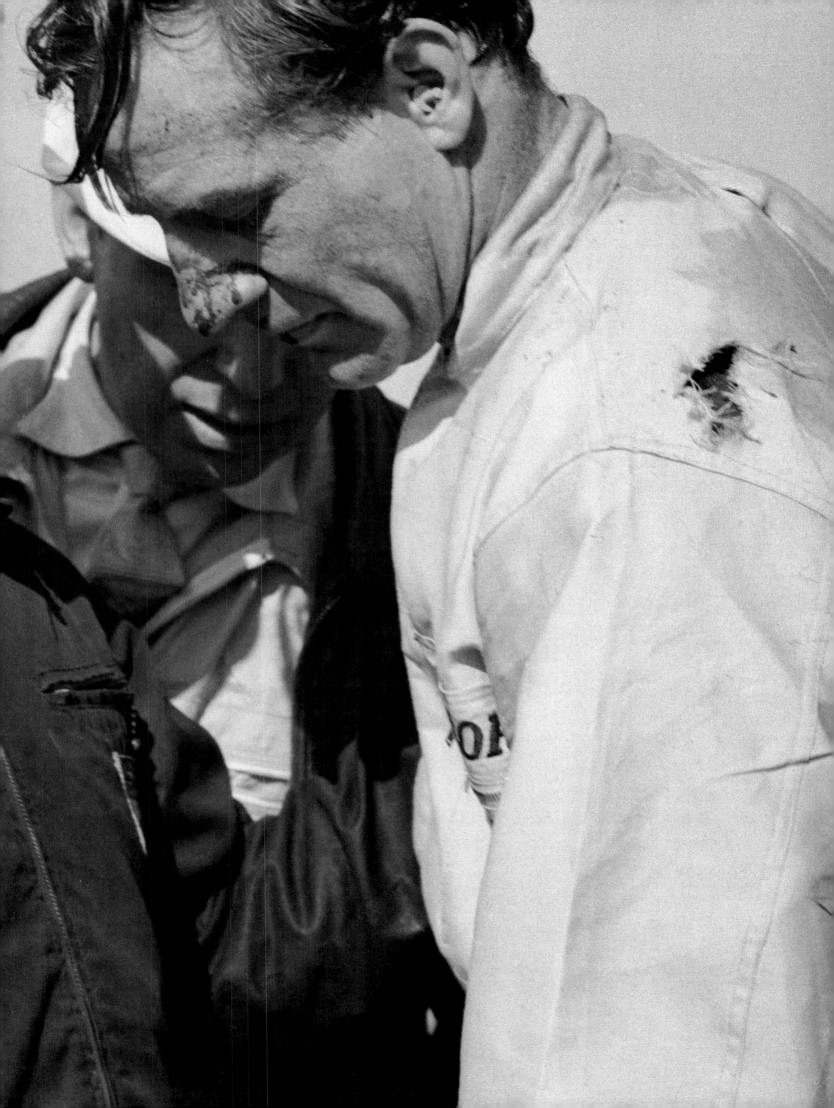

The Price

THE PRICE of motor racing is wrecked machinery, fright, blood, and sometimes life itself. On preceding pages five cars were wrecked in four separate accidents, but no one was seriously hurt.

Now on the next eight pages a single accident is seen in detail. Two cars have brushed together coming out of a fast turn. At more than 100 miles per hour, both go out of control and crash into the hillside (right). As other cars speed through the smoke and cluttered road, the driver of the burning car lies on the hill just above the flames, where the impact threw him. A stretcher from the ambulance has been hurried across the road and moved up to him. Behind the ambulance, the driver of the second car wanders about dazedly. In the confusion of the crackling flames, of racers roaring through the smoke and gloom, no one knows clearly what has happened or why.

Reaction

TWO FERRARIS speed past the burning, upside-down wreck. Neither driver knows what has happened or who is hurt, perhaps dead. The head of the rookie driver, trailing, is screwed sideways, eyes trying to penetrate the smoke and steam. The veteran driver stares straight ahead. Later he will answer in a flat voice, "What did it do to me? Nothing. Do I sound callous? I used to go to pieces. I'd see an accident like that and feel so weak inside that I wanted to quit, to stop the car and get out. I could hardly make myself go past it.

"But I'm older now. When I see something like that, something really horrible, I put my foot down, because I know everyone else is lifting his."

The procession has crossed the road and is moving toward the ambulance. The stretcher bearers, with jobs to do, hurry forward. Everyone else is in a daze. The uninjured driver strides before the group without knowing how he got there, nor what he is doing. A photographer gapes, forgetting to take pictures. A spectator carries the helmet of the driver who is on the stretcher, momentarily believing this an important task. Two flag marshals and a gendarme tramp about the road, and only the nurse, looking back over her shoulder, seems worried about other cars hurtling forward through the gloom.

Reaction (2)

THE UNINJURED DRIVER, Trevor Taylor, is limp. It has been that close. He stares at the proffered cigarette unable to move. Across the road, the other driver, Willy Mairesse, lies in pain. One shoe has been ripped off, his pants legs are gone, his face is bloody. He lifts a gloved hand, tries to say something.

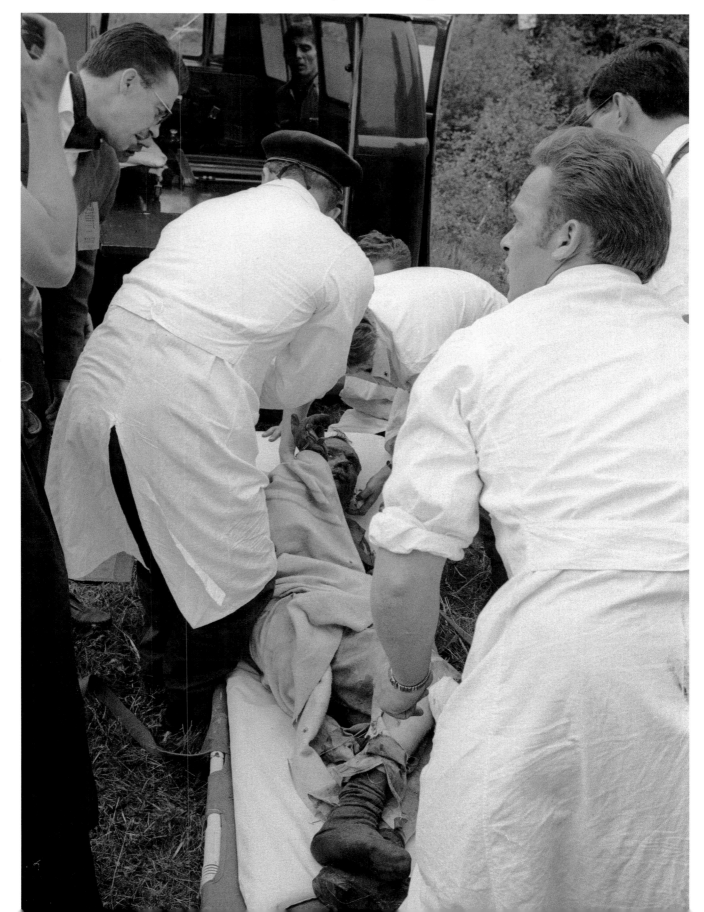

The Race Goes On

TWO CARS and a telephone pole have been destroyed. One driver has lost three teeth and some skin. Perhaps both drivers have lost some verve. The fourth-place car moves up to finish second. It was not a bad crash, as crashes go. Both drivers have been very, very lucky.

The race goes on. The race always goes on, whether the accident has been "not a bad crash" or the worst possible one. Below, at Monza, the Porsche of Dan Gurney speeds past the wreckage of a Ferrari which has just killed sixteen people, including its driver.

Why Do They Race

Wolfgang von Trips:

I SAT WITH Wolfgang von Trips for the last time after practice the eve of the 1961 Italian Grand Prix.

Behind the pits at Monza there are shops and restaurants under the trees. We sat down on the terrace of a café. I ordered a *caffe latte*, and Trips ordered tea. People kept stopping to congratulate him or to wish him luck, and he answered cordially in various languages. We talked. He seemed not so much nervous as feeling the strain. Everyone expected him to be world champion, and probably he himself was ready to be, but he was too well-bred to let this show. As we talked, I remembered sitting with him at another café in Belgium some years before, and he told me the story of his first crash at Monza. He told it just the way it is reprinted below, simply, a story impossible to forget; and as he finished, a girl came up and said, "You don't remember me, do you?" Standing, Trips took both her hands and said, "Let me look deep into your eyes." She gazed at him doubtfully. "How could I ever forget such eyes," he said with a gentle smile. "How could I ever forget *you*." I was charmed, as the girl was; he was a courtly, brave young man. He could relive a terrible crash: the expression in his eyes had showed that he was reliving it, but a moment later he was able to forget and to flirt. I liked him.

Now, on the eve of the 1961 Italian Grand Prix, we talked and sipped our drinks, and then I thanked him and went back to my hotel in Milan and wrote the article reprinted below. I remember wondering if Trips would like it; at length, I decided he would. Of course, he never saw it. It appeared in the sports section of the *New York Times* the next morning, Sunday, about the hour (because of the time difference) that the engines were being revved up at Monza. Before most New Yorkers had finished their first cups of coffee, Trips was dead.

By ROBERT DALEY
Special to the *New York Times*

MONZA, Italy, Sept. 9—The Ferraris of Count Wolfgang von Trips, Ricardo Rodriguez, Richie Ginther and Phil Hill have qualified one, two, three, four for tomorrow's 267-mile Grand Prix of Italy.

This has been up to now predominantly a Ferrari year, and a von Trips year. Von Trips, could, in fact, clinch the driver's world championship tomorrow if he were to win this race and Phil Hill were to finish no better than fourth. Von Trips has 33 points after six of eight scheduled races. Hill has 29.

But this circuit—and memory—may be against von Trips. Hill has set lap records at Monza every year since 1958. And last year, winning this race, he became the first American to win a major Grand Prix in forty years.

Hill is confident here. Von Trips may not be. The German not only has never won here, he has twice been dragged out of terrible wrecks, both times crashing in the long right-hand turn just past the pits where the road turns into the forest.

Von Trips was born on May 4, 1928, heir to the family castle and lands near Cologne. He began driving a motorcycle in trials and cross-country events in 1948. He had no money and little time. He was working with his hands on a farm in order to qualify for an agricultural degree. In Germany, no man may inherit land unless he is a qualified farmer.

A few years later, Trips acquired a battered old Porsche which he entered in two rallies, winning a class victory in one of them. Then one of the Porsche's pistons burned out.

"I had no money," von Trips recalls. "I went to the factory and tried to get them to give me an old piston. Instead they offered me a car to race in the Mille Miglia.

"I said: 'The Mille Miglia? What's that?'"

It was explained to him that this was a 1,000-mile sports car race over the open roads of Italy, one of the fastest, most dangerous and most famous races in the world.

"I had never driven a car over 85 miles an hour in my life at that time," von Trips said, "but I said to them, 'Of course I'd like to drive in the race.'"

This was in 1954 and von Trips is still amazed and thrilled when he thinks of his performance that day. "I had never seen the roads before, nor driven the car before, nor raced before, but I didn't make one single mistake and I won a class victory."

Mistakes were to come, plenty of them.

For two years Trips drove occasional races for Porsche and Mercedes. Then, in 1956, he was asked by Enzo Ferrari to come here to Monza to try out for the Ferrari team.

The Ferrari's steering broke in the Curva Grande at 120 miles an hour. The car shot off into the forest, straight at a great tree. "I saw the tree coming at me. There was nothing I could do. I said to myself: You're dead, Trips."

That first tree lopped off one side of the Ferrari, and a second tree amputated the other side. The wheelless, naked chassis dug into the ground nose-first and flipped end over end, over and over.

Trips was thrown out. "I lay on the ground and thought: 'is this what it's like to be dead?' And then I realized I was smelling the dirt and I said to myself, 'Trips, you're not dead.'"

Ferrari sent Trips back to Germany.

Trips was so sore he could hardly move; but two weeks later in Berlin in his own cars he won two races. He drove them with his right arm strapped to his side, shifting and steering with his left hand.

"Ferrari said that if I wanted to race that badly, I could race for him, and he sent me a contract."

In the next two seasons von Trips' career was marked by accidents. He crashed all over the world. He became known around the race circuits as von Krash. In the Italian Grand Prix in 1958 (at Monza again), he drove his Ferrari up the back of Harry Schell's BRM on the first lap, and both cars crashed. Schell was only shaken up, but Trips' leg was smashed.

Ferrari sent him back to Germany again. His contract was not renewed.

The following spring, driving a Porsche in the Monaco Grand Prix, Trips collided with Cliff Allison's Ferrari, both cars crashing. Pulled from the wreck upset and shaken, Trips mumbled: "I don't even have to be on the Ferrari team to wreck Ferraris."

That might have been the end of him in big-time racing, but he loves racing too much, and wouldn't be stopped. He kept asking Ferrari to take him back, and finally Ferrari did.

This year there have been no crashes. Von Trips says this is pure luck. "The line between maximum speed and crashing is so thin," he says, "so thin."

But talking to him it is clear that he is wiser than he was, more experienced and more careful. Many of his crashes had been on the first or second lap. He had been that impetuous.

Von Trips is single. "I am married to one of these," he says, pointing to a Ferrari. He speaks English, French and Italian in addition to German, all not only fluently, but without accent. "I have no hobbies," he says intensely. "Racing is my hobby."

(Trips said one other thing that last evening at Monza. Talking about the thin line between maximum speed and crashing, he had said abruptly, "It could happen tomorrow. That's the thing about this business. You never know." As I wrote the article, I thought about this remark for some time, then decided to leave it out. Too melodramatic. Not significant.)

In Defense of Car Racing:

THE NEXT DAY, September 10, 1961, during the second lap of the Grand Prix of Italy, Trips' blood-red Ferrari slewed off the road at 150 miles per hour. It climbed a five-foot-high earthen embankment, brushed for the briefest possible instant a wire fence restraining part of the crowd, then bounded tumbling and spinning down the bank and back into the road again. Dead were fifteen spectators who had pressed against the fence—and Trips.

That night the Monza circuit was closed off, the wrecked race car was impounded by police, the dead were claimed, and the world was left to brood. Why do men race? Why do other men watch? Will there be no end to these accidents? And, if not, can motor racing be allowed to continue?

Phil Hill, winner of both the race and the 1961 drivers' world championship, brooded too. Newspaper reports the next day irritated him; most were garbled and foolish. He studied the photographs and tried to think out exactly what did happen. A call came through from London from a reporter. "Too bad about your teammate getting killed," the man said. "Tell me, do you have any hobbies? Do you smoke or drink?"

Hill was in the lobby of the hotel still muttering, when a friend, myself, said to him, "Are you going to quit, Phil?"—hoping he would say "yes," hoping that he, at least, would not end up a bundle in the road like Trips.

"I don't know," he snapped. "I haven't made up my mind yet."

A little later he came over and sat down. He began to talk. "There are more 'don'ts' than 'do's' in the business," he said. "Trips violated a 'don't' by trying to occupy a space already partially occupied by Clark's Lotus. It's horrible in a way. But in another way it's not so horrible. After all, everybody dies. Isn't it a fine thing that Trips died doing something he loved, without any suffering, without any warning? I think Trips would rather be dead than not race, don't you?"

"What are you going to do, Phil?"

He thought a moment and then said, "When I love motor racing less, my own life will become worth more to me, and I will be less willing to risk it."

Motor racing is full of horror, and one never gets used to it. It knots up the stomach so that you can't eat or sleep. You toss all night and with the first light of dawn come tiredly awake again to brood some more. Trips had raced by the grandstand at 160 miles per hour, bold, proud, alive. A few seconds later—how can this be? The mind cannot comprehend it, nor let it go either. I told Hill now that I had had enough. I was going back to Paris to see some tennis matches, to lose myself in them if I could.

Hill said, "Tennis. Yes, tennis is a very dangerous game. The players risk all sorts of terrible things: sprained ankles, twisted knees, tennis elbow." His voice was filled with bitterness, as if he recognized that for others there existed a safe, comfortable world from which he, for some reason, had been excluded.

NEITHER HILL nor anyone else ever expressed regret for the fifteen customers who died with Trips, beyond noting that there would now be much agitation to abolish motor racing again. This reaction is normal. The personal tragedy of Trips overshadowed the destruction of other, unknown people. In addition, the death of Trips seemed to them not an accident, but still another human sacrifice to the voracious god of fast cars.

The spectators died the way men die in a burning building or a plane crash; they had the bad luck to be in the wrong spot at the wrong time. There was no inevitability to their deaths until the instant that the race car was on top of them, whereas Trips' death had been inevitable from the moment he climbed into his first race car, grinned happily, and made the engine roar.

There was nothing new in the Monza

accident. Motor racing has been killing drivers since 1898, about as soon as men were able to force the speed of their rickety machines over 30 miles per hour. It has been killing spectators since 1903, when the Paris-Madrid race was stopped at Bordeaux after about a dozen people, including some drivers, died in several different accidents. The average speed of that 1903 race was 65 miles per hour. Hill won at Monza at 130.

So death in motor racing—both to drivers and to spectators—is inevitable. Let there be no mistake about this. Of the sixteen drivers who started the 1958 season in the Grand Prix of Monaco, seven are now dead and two, Moss and Cliff Allison, were so badly broken in crashes that they will probably never race again. On a lower level than Grand Prix racing, the toll would be much less. This is a trade in which skill does not protect a man. It exposes him more than ever by bringing him closer and closer to the absolute limit.

As for crowd deaths, there was a bad accident in 1961 at Monza, 1958 in Cuba, 1957 in the Mille Miglia, 1955 at Le Mans, 1953 in Argentina, and so on. About 125 people were killed in just these accidents— but it must be pointed out that the races in question were watched by over ten million people. If that many had spent the day doing anything at all—even climbing a flight of stairs—as many or more probably would have died anyway.

People are, after all, people. They make mistakes. They have accidents. This is horrible, but nothing can be done about it.

Each time there is a motor racing crash involving spectators, the cause of that particular crash is, as far as men are able to do so, eliminated. The Mille Miglia was stopped as an open-road race, the Le Mans circuit was redone at a cost of several millions of dollars, and in Argentina, a week after the 1953 crash, dictator Juan Perón stationed men with machine guns to hold back the crowd.

Motor racing always does what it can, but it cannot do a one-hundred percent job because the behavior of a racing car out of control is not only unpredictable, it is often absolutely incredible.

In 1960, in the Grand Prix of Belgium, the Lotus of Alan Stacey went off the road on the inside of a 120-mile-an-hour curve, climbed a waist-high embankment, penetrated ten feet of tightly interlaced hedges, and dropped into a field. The crash killed no one except Stacey; the point is that the Lotus ended up in what men would have called the safest single spot on the circuit— the inside of a turn, where tremendous forces push a car outwards, and behind the embankment and the hedges.

Trips' car, in effect, lightly sideswiped the fence at Monza, then was flung back into the road again. What flung it back, altered its course at 150 miles per hour? Certainly not the flimsy wire fence it struck. It is easy to blame the race organizers for permitting an embankment there that was sloping rather than sheer. The slope sent the Ferrari up to the fence. But a sheer embankment might have caught the nose of the Ferrari like a line drive and made it disintegrate, spraying pieces into the crowd and killing even more. It is impossible to know for sure.

Any man who has seen a few of these crashes knows that the crowd can never be made entirely safe unless it is moved so far back and protected by so many walls and ditches that all drama will be eliminated as effectively as all danger. If this were done, spectators wouldn't come, and motor racing would soon stop.

MORE PEOPLE watch motor racing than any other sport—not only in Europe, but in America as well. Motor racing in its various forms (stock-car racing, road racing, track racing) brings out more Americans every year than baseball or any other game, and in Europe crowds of 300,000 at Le Mans, the Nürburgring, and elsewhere are common.

It has often been said that people come to see death, and possibly a few do come for that reason only, particularly at track races. But surely it is more accurate to say that men come in order to experience vicarious danger and vicarious bravery. By pressing close to all that speed, ears assaulted by the noise, the whole body shaken by it, Mr. Average-Timid-Soul can imagine himself for an afternoon a dashing race driver controlling peril, laughing at death, brave beyond belief.

There is much more to it. Nearly every race is fraught with suspense. Even when one car is far in front, as Hill was at Monza, the avid fan is tingling with tension. He worries about Hill's car: three other Ferraris have broken down, will Hill's last? The fan might also worry about Hill's life—to a man close to the track, the danger is horribly apparent.

The average car race is also what the Germans call a "Volksfest," a grand outing for the entire family. The shortest of races lasts two hours, in which case it usually is preceded by others. The longest of them lasts eight or twelve or twenty-four hours. Whole families come bringing picnic lunches, umbrellas, radios—it's like a day at the beach.

They watch the race a while, then eat, talk, snooze, then watch the race some more, wandering from corner to corner to observe techniques and absorb the spectacle. Many emotions are touched at every race, even the race at Monza. Thousands of people went home that night without even knowing of the Trips tragedy. To them it had been a pleasant day in the forest watching a race. And, of course, to the German driver Wolfgang Siedel, weeping for Trips in the paddock as dusk fell, the Grand Prix of Italy had been something else altogether.

In any case, no adult comes to a car race without being aware of the danger, in the same way that no man boards an airplane without being aware of the danger. The odds against you are very small but they do exist. You know it, and you take your chances. To say that motor racing should be abolished because spectators were killed in the past and will be killed in the future is to be unrealistic. Why ban just car racing? Why not ban mountain climbing, bullfighting, bike racing, hunting, fishing, boating, swimming? Why not ban airliners, trains, crossing the street, and Sunday outings in the family sedan?

The question most often asked about drivers is: why do they race?

There are answers to this question which are deep and obscure. Hill touches on them when he remarks, "It depends how much glorification your ego needs. If it needs enough, the danger of racing goes right out the window, you don't even think of that."

There are also the obvious answers. Men race for the pleasure, the money, and the adulation.

There is pleasure in the blur of trees rushing by, in the terrific pressure of the seat in the small of a man's back. There is, above all, pleasure in controlling a car in a turn, loading up the centrifugal force, accelerating just so much and no more, making the tail slide out just enough to point the nose into the next straight, then stomping the accelerator into the floor. Racing is fun, make no mistake.

And on the economic level it pays well. All top Grand Prix drivers earn $20,000 or more a year in starting money and prizes. Many a young man has got into the sport because it is, in Europe, socially "in," and because he thought that as a driver he could sway girls, only to find himself trapped in it later by the money. What else could he do to earn so much? Most drivers are men unsuited to offices or factories. Once they get used to the money they have no choice but to keep racing.

It may be that the biggest appeal of all is the adulation. Grand Prix racing has hundreds of men and girls of all ages who follow the cars and drivers everywhere and who worship openly at the shrine. Drivers see a romantic, reflected image of themselves in the eyes of these people. There is awe and the most naked kind of admiration there. At times the risk of racing must seem a trivial thing, compared with the importance which these people make a driver feel. As he settles into his cramped machine, revving the engine up and down, tense, eyes glued on the starter's flag, the crowd gulping with excitement—at such a moment a driver feels himself a god. What is danger next to that?

Motor racing is the cruelest sport. It is also the most brilliant, because it is man wrestling with his demons on the edge of the infinite. It cannot be made safe; it can only be stopped. To stop it might prevent fourteen or fifteen deaths each year—not very many in a world like ours—at a permanent cost of all that spectacle and noise, glamour and heroism, love and fear. The world would be a dimmer place without the fast cars and the men who race them. Would it be a better one?

Epilogue

WHEN THE FOREGOING was written I was thirty-one years old and still in possession of some of my illusions, not all. Trips' death had one other effect: it made me aware of how fond I had become of Phil Hill. This was a burden, for in the Grand Prix arena in which both of us stood it did not pay to become fond of anyone. Phil had got me that interview with Ferrari, though I hadn't known him well at the time, and hadn't really asked him to do it. From then on I was in his camp, and in each race I worried about him—more now than ever.

He had long been the one from whom I got most of my information. The financial aspects of a driver's life. Which of his colleagues were fastest. Much else as well. Every reporter (every detective too, I was to learn later) must find an informant who is in close himself, and who will bring the reporter in with him. A reporter is not obliged to find a hundred, or a dozen, or even four or five sources. He just has to find one he can trust who can tell him what he needs to know. Or at least that is what I felt then, and still feel, about the reporting trade. I checked out Phil's information often enough. I never found him wrong.

Most of what he said was quotable, sometimes shockingly so, making him for me, and for the *New York Times*, marvelous copy. His conversation always reflected his feelings, and he seemed as ambivalent about car racing as I was. He loved it and feared it both. Of one of his Ferrari teammates he once said: "If he lives, I'll be surprised," and that particular driver, Ricardo Rodriguez, twenty years old, was dead within the year. Of owners he said: "Most of them see us as funny little psychopaths who sooner or later become too scared to stick our shoe in it."

Once in the Grand Prix of Belgium in heavy rain a number of cars went off the road. Phil went past ambulances on every lap. When the race ended he pulled into the pits exhausted, dispirited, soaked, and looked up at me and said: "Well, who got killed?"

He was not married, did not think a racing driver had a right to marry, and did not marry himself until his racing days were over. He would look at the drivers' wives sitting on pit counters working stopwatches, apparently calm, apparently unaware of what their husbands were doing, and this amazed him. He thought these women must all be stupid.

He was not easy to know. Although he let me in close some days, he rebuffed me on others, but then he treated everybody this way. Most of us thought him an enigma, and around restaurant tables the conversation was often about Hill. Who was Phil Hill, really?

It was a question that demanded multiple answers, most of which elude me to this day, but if anything ever happened to him, I came to feel, I would never be able to go to another car race.

AS I WATCHED all these young men die, it became harder and harder to see their sport as sport. What they did had nothing to do with laughter or love or pleasure or even pain. Its excitement, it seemed to me, was based on the tendency of human beings to make mistakes, and on the extreme fragility of human life.

Grand Prix racing was a world in which skill did not protect a man, it put him closer to the hole. Drivers made a thousand judgments in every race, any one of which, if only slightly inaccurate, would send the car off the road at great speed. Which, depending on how solid the object it eventually hit, could kill him. One year we were treated to a posthumous world champion. His name was Jochen Rindt. With only one European race left he had already clinched the title. The crash virtually decapitated him.

I was having trouble comprehending all this. Why were we willing to go on with it? Why were we permitted to go on with it? One day I wondered in print how motor racing could survive the loss of so many of its stars in so short a time. The sport was in the process of devouring itself. Drivers big enough to draw crowds did not emerge overnight, it took years, whereas to kill one took only an instant, and each time this happened a replacement came in who was a nobody, and who would remain one a good long time. No entertainment medium could prosper very long under conditions like that.

How long, I asked myself, my readers too, could the sport continue to exist?

And as my view of motor racing changed, so in subtle ways did my very character. I felt myself becoming pessimistic, even morbid, and did not like myself for it. I counted the cars every time around. Whose funeral would be next?

Such macabre thoughts were with me always, and to some extent have stayed.

THESE DAYS Michael Schumacher, who has won now more world championships than Fangio, has been known to butt rival cars off the road at speed. A driver who tried this in those years risked killing himself as well as the driver he butted. The difference is that Schumacher races on small closed courses that are as manicured and antiseptic as designers can make them, circuits bordered by escape roads, by vast beaches of sand, and in some places by mountains of old tires. There is virtually nothing left to hit. A driver can go off almost anywhere with impunity. The famous old circuits are used rarely now or never. Those that survive at all have been cut way down. The 14-mile Nürburgring has been cut to 2.9 miles. The 8.7-mile Spa circuit now measures 4.3. The cars may be safer too, more solidly constructed, lower to the ground and running on great fat tires. They have wings that hold them down. They have on-board computers, power steering. Gear changing is automatic. They carry black boxes like airliners. Schumacher is said to earn $25 million a year. But at the time of which I write, $25,000 was a big year. Endorsement contracts were scarce, because advertisers had no interest in building a campaign around a young man who might not live out the week, much less the season. Moss, who was a tremendous star in England, got a few endorsements, as did Phil Hill the year he won the world championship. Most of the others, nothing.

I WATCHED eleven Grand Prix de Monaco in all. It was the first I ever saw, as I have said, and the last as well.

With my photographer's brassard, I was allowed to move anywhere I chose (on the other circuits also), a freedom which—now that the sport has become such big, big business, making for, potentially, such big, big lawsuits—is no longer permitted. I was on my feet and moving, watching the race mostly through lenses, for nearly three hours, and I got close enough to be physically assaulted by the noise and speed. If I gave up worrying about personal safety and leaned out over the street, I could get close-ups no one else had tried for. And I saw exactly how dangerous, even here, this sport could be.

I always watched part of the time at the chicane, where the cars came out of the tunnel under Loew's Hotel, and then wriggled up onto what normally was a promenade around the harbor. Here they were slowed enough for me to photograph drivers' faces as they wrenched the wheel first left, then right. In addition I could try for race cars in the foreground and yachts in the background, often with girls in bikinis watching avidly from their decks—a nice juxtaposition, I thought. At the chicane, I also knew, there had been interesting pileups in the past. But no one had ever been hurt there prior to the crash I am about to describe, and hardly anyone had ever been hurt anywhere else on this circuit either, for the Grand Prix de Monaco was and is too slow a race. Only the other races killed drivers, we all believed. It took decades for the winning car here to average over eighty miles an hour, and even today they barely exceed ninety. For a race car that is creeping. At such relative slowness the car can always be stopped before great damage is done. Almost always.

In the absence of great speeds and danger, the Grand Prix de Monaco was, and for most spectators still is, celebrated mostly for its setting. It is the race through the streets. The race around the houses. There are those who call it the most cherished and exciting of all the races—but the excitement does not have much to do with the race itself, for there is no place to pass, so that nearly always the race is not a race but a parade.

The excitement is something else. Monaco is an enclave of riches, and during race week all this wealth and luxury is there to see: the women in jewelry, the elegant girls, the curbs lined with Rolls Royces, Ferraris, Lamborghinis, the crowded lobbies, the parties. While outside in the street those brilliant, uncouth machines ravage the silence of the town. The air so electric that one sometimes finds it difficult to breathe. A unique race in a unique setting.

A race to be watched, if possible, while sipping champagne.

I watched nine of these Monaco Grand Prix, and nothing bad happened. Then the bill was presented here too.

A Ferrari driver named Lorenzo Bandini paid it. I watched him pay it.

It was late in the race. Bandini was perhaps tired. That he had become slightly less accurate in placing his machine is certain. He came though the chicane cleanly enough but once on the harbor front never got properly straightened out. The barrier there was a row of straw bales braced with telephone poles. A homemade affair designed to keep errant cars from plunging into the harbor. Nothing steel or scientific, as now. The Ferrari's left wheels touched this barrier, then clawed their way up it spewing hay, and as the car climbed it capsized.

Then it was in the air upside down, flying.

It flew quite far.

If it had flown into the water, where frogmen waited to fish drivers out, Bandini might be alive today, but it didn't. Instead, it came down on the pavement on top of him. There was an audible whoosh, like a giant expelling all his air, and then it burst into flames. Sometimes the flames parted and Bandini's helmet could be seen, pressed sideways under the rim of the burning car.

I stood in horror, my cameras forgotten, while the flag marshals tried to get the fire out and succeeded for a moment, during which they half lifted up the car, but when the flames burst forth again they dropped it and jumped away. Other men came with other extinguishers. It seemed to take forever. Probably it lasted three or four minutes. A long time if you are burning to death. When the fire was reduced to a sputter, they again tried to lift the car, but

again the flames blazed up, and again they dropped it back on Bandini and ran. All this time the race continued. The other cars kept coming through. They were slowed by the smoke and flames and hay and foam, but they kept coming through.

At a certain point I gave myself a lecture. Take the picture, I told myself. But I'm watching a man die, I told myself. I don't care, I told myself. Set the aperture, set the speed, and take the picture. You're a professional. Take it, take it.

So finally I took several. One photo from that series later hung in museums (The Art Institute of Chicago, The Baltimore Museum, the New York Gallery of Modern Art) as part of a Man in Sport exhibition. Which proves, as is true of many of the great photos of the world, that I happened to be standing in that particular spot. Nothing much else.

THE DEATH of Bandini must have marked me more than I knew. Although I have been a professional writer all my adult life, I never described it in prose until I wrote the words you are reading. Sometimes I have asked myself why. There had been many previous deaths—too many, as I have said—but this one marked me in a different and more profound way than all previous ones. Suddenly, finally, I had had enough. I didn't want to see anything like that again. I couldn't bear to go back, not to Monaco, not to anywhere else the fast cars ran.

Twelve years passed before this emotion dimmed enough for me to accept another assignment to the Monaco Grand Prix. There was international TV now. The drivers had become rich, their faces known far and wide. When not in their cars they hid out in trailers like film stars. The same electricity was in the air, however, and although for me much of the romance was missing, perhaps gone forever, still everyone else seemed to feel it. The crowds, I saw, stirred to the spectacle in the same old way. The setting had not changed either: the parties, the yachts, the fancy motor cars, the girls in bikinis. In limitless amounts the champagne still flowed.

But for me The Cruel Sport was over. I have never gone back and do not think I ever will.

Photo Identifications

The photos in this book were made between 1959 and 1967, at sixteen circuits in nine countries, and also at the Ferrari factory in Maranello, Italy; at the Cooper factory, Surbiton, England; and at the home of Olivier Gendebien at Perthes-en-Gatinais, near Paris. Many of the captions that follow have been updated to 2005

Cover photo: The start at Spa-Francorchamps circuit, Belgian G. P. 1962.

Front endpaper: Lorenzo Bandini and admirers, Monaco, May 1964.

Rear endpaper: The upside down Ferrari, burning, Bandini trapped under it. Monaco, May 7, 1967.

Title page photo: Tony Maggs in a Cooper, Dutch G. P. 1962.

Page numbers:

1: Jack Brabham mobbed by photographers and officials moments after winning Dutch G. P., June 6, 1960.

2: Jim Clark. Picture made Sept. 16, 1962, Monza, Italy. Born March 4, 1936, Clark won 25 of 72 Grand Prix races, two world championships, and, in 1965, the Indianapolis 500. He was killed at Hockenheim, West Germany, April 6, 1968, during a relatively unimportant Formula 2 race. Went off the road into a tree. I have seen no satisfactory explanation for this crash. Rival drivers were bewildered. One, Chris Amon, said: "If Clark wasn't safe, what chance do the rest of us have?" Three other major drivers were killed that same year.

4: Graham Hill: born Feb. 15, 1929; picture made June 3, 1962, Monaco. In 1968 Hill won his second world championship. He also won Indianapolis in 1966. By 1975 he had developed a car of his own manufacture which, driven by protégés, was never able to finish higher than fifth. On Nov. 29 of that year, piloting his own plane back from tests on the Paul Ricard circuit near Marseilles, he crashed in dense fog on a golf course near Elstree, England, and was killed, along with five others—the protégé Tony Brise, three mechanics, and an engineer. The airport he was trying to reach was near his house but had no radar, no runway lights, and a minimal navigation system. Luton, a major airport, was close and had all these things, but he chose not to go there. Afterwards there were lawsuits, trouble with his insurance; his wife was left with severe financial problems and had to scale way back. Their son Damon, born in 1960, fifteen years old when his father died, won the world championship in 1996 driving a Williams. After the season for unknown reasons he was fired by Frank Williams, the owner. He lasted another three years in inferior cars, then retired.

6: Jo Bonnier born Jan. 31, 1930. Picture made Aug. 4, 1962, the Nürburgring, Germany. Driving a Lola, Bonnier was killed at Le Mans in June 1972.

9: Olivier Gendebien born Jan. 12, 1924; picture made Jan. 7, 1963, Perthes-en-Gatinais, France. Retired 1962 after winning Le Mans for the fourth time. Died 1998.

11: Brabham born April 2, 1926; picture made May 19, 1962, Zandvoort, Holland Brabham won the world championship three times, the final time in a car of his own manufacture. As an old man he was knighted by Queen Elizabeth II.

12: Ferrari driver Ricardo Rodriguez born Feb. 14, 1942, killed Nov. 1, 1962, during practice for the Mexican Grand Prix. Picture made at Zandvoort, Holland, May 20, 1962. His brother Pedro, two years older, was killed driving in a minor sports car race in Germany on July 11, 1971.

13: Maurice Trintignant born Oct. 30, 1917; picture made Aug. 5, 1962, the Nürburgring. Trintignant is at present 87 years old.

14: Bruce McLaren born Aug. 30, 1937; picture made June 2, 1962, before practice for Monaco G. P. He was killed June 2, 1970, testing one of his own cars at Goodwood. The McLaren marque went on without him and is one of the most successful that has ever raced. Its various drivers, in machines powered by engines from Honda, Tag, Mercedes, etc., have won eleven world championships.

16: Wolfgang von Trips born May 4, 1928, killed Sept. 10, 1961, Grand Prix of Italy. Picture made May 24, 1959, the Targa Florio, Sicily.

18: Giancarlo Baghetti born Dec. 25, 1934; picture made May 19, 1962, Zandvoort. Died of cancer, age 60, Nov. 27, 1995.

20: John Surtees born Feb. 11, 1934; picture made May 13, 1961, Monaco.

22: Willy Mairesse born Oct. 1, 1928; picture made Sept. 15, 1962, Monza. In June 1968 Mairesse crashed at Le Mans. He was 15 days in a coma, suffered from headaches from then on. He was hospitalized in January of the following year and again in July. He committed suicide Sept. 2, 1969. He was 41.

23: Harry Schell was killed at Silverstone in practice May 13, 1960, at the age of 39; this photo was made at Lisbon, Aug. 22, 1959.

25: Richie Ginther born Aug. 5, 1930; picture made July 20, 1962, Aintree. Died of heart failure Sept. 20, 1989.

26: Dan Gurney born April 13, 1931; picture made Aug. 23, 1959, Lisbon.

27: Gurney—taken May 19, 1962, Zandvoort.

28: Tony Brooks born Feb. 25, 1932; picture made May 9, 1959, Monaco.

31: Innes Ireland born June 12, 1930, died age 63, Oct. 22, 1993; picture made May 19, 1962, Zandvoort.

33: Phil Hill born April 20, 1927; picture made June 3, 1962, Monaco. After retiring from competition, Hill, with a partner, opened a shop in Santa Monica for the restoration of classic cars, doing much of the work himself. He sometimes wrote articles for the motor racing press. When his son, Derek, born in 1975, wanted to become a racing driver, Hill pushed the boy's career as much as he could. He also attended Grand Prix races, and the functions and galas that went with them, at which, more and more as the years passed, he was treated as a God.

38: Stirling Moss born Sept. 17, 1929; picture made May 29, 1960, Monaco.

39: Moss—taken Sept. 16, 1962, Monza. Sir Stirling was knighted by Queen Elizabeth II in 1999.

46: Clark. Picture made at Trenton, N.J., 1964. Clark was there for a 100-mile Indianapolis-type race in which he broke down.

53: Jackie Stewart. Picture made at Belgium Grand Prix, June 12, 1966. The English driver Roy Salvadori, who survived those years, though barely, told the author in 2004 that Stewart was the first driver who dared say, in effect: "This is insane, this is crazy," and to demand that safety measures be taken. "All of us knew that what we were doing was ridiculously dangerous," Salvadori told me, "but none of us was willing to say so very loudly." It was Stewart who demanded seat belts and fireproof clothing. More and more measures were added, though slowly, leading eventually to the sanitizing of all the circuits. The mass killing of this handful of young men went on until at least 1980, when three were killed and one paralyzed in four different races. Stewart himself was the reigning driver of his time, as Clark was before him, and Moss and Fangio before that. Stewart raced in 99 Grand Prix,

won 27 of them and was world champion three times. When his teammate François Cevert was killed in practice at Watkins Glen on Oct. 6, 1973, the second fatality that year, Stewart withdrew from the next day's race, and presently announced his retirement. He was 34.

59: Monza, Italy, Sept. 15, 1962. This museum is in a field just behind the paddock, and in front of the straight leading to the south curve. This straight can be seen upper left. Most of the old car museums of Europe, and there are many, contain old racing cars too. The best museums are at Turin and at the Mercedes-Benz factory near Stuttgart.

60: Nürburgring, Aug. 4, 1962. Hermann Lang, Europemeister in 1939, about to do a demonstration lap in the 1939 Mercedes after practice, the day before the German G. P.

61: Monaco, June 3, 1962. The knee-high-to-a-photographer Lotus.

62, top: Bonnier, BRM, Monaco 1959.

62, bottom: Phil Hill, Ferrari, during 1960 French G. P., Reims. It was in this car that Hill won the Italian Grand Prix, the last European race that season, and the last victory ever for a front engined car.

63, top: Carroll Shelby in the 1959 Aston Martin, waiting for start of the Portuguese G. P. at Lisbon. The Aston Martin factory had won glory and publicity in sports car racing, but its Grand Prix car shown here took too long to get ready. By the time it appeared that year, the trend was to rear-engined cars much lighter and thinner than itself. The factory saw that it was too late with this design. Declining to pay the costs of a new design, it abandoned the sport altogether.

63, bottom: McLaren's narrow cockpit, Belgium,1963. Since the Spa circuit is the fastest, it is also the place where streamlining pays off most. Even so, McLaren's cockpit seems rather too narrow.

65: Aintree, England, July 20, 1962. Mechanics adjust the Lotus of Clark which was to win the British G. P. the next day.

67: Enzo Ferrari never goes to races, but sometimes watches testing of his cars. This picture was made at Modena in April 1959 during the testing of a Ferrari sports car by Phil Hill. Ferrari was then 61. The tests were made at the Modena airport, light planes and gliders taking off from grass landing strips inside the roughly rectangular road circuit which surrounds the airport. Ferrari died Aug. 14, 1988, aged 90.

68: Outside the Ferrari factory at Maranello, Aug. 9, 1962.

71: The racing car assembly line, Aug. 9, 1962. Pictures inside the factory are not permitted by order of Commendatore Ferrari. Journalists are not permitted inside either, except on rare occasions; Ferrari himself once had shown me around. On the day this photo was made, Phil Hill arranged for me to be shown through the factory again. Ferrari was not there. My guide was called away. I slipped a Kodak Retina camera out of my pocket and hurriedly snapped some photos. Some mechanics saw me. When the guide came back, they told him. "Did you take any photos?" I was asked coldly. My visit was terminated. When I told Phil, he laughed. He was quitting Ferrari very soon, and did not care. Few pictures such as this one exist; thank a big pocket, a small folding camera, and Phil Hill.

73: The Cooper Garage, Surbiton, England, Sept. 25, 1962.

75: John Cooper, enthusiastic and talkative, led me through his place. "Can I take a picture?" I asked hopefully. "Take a hundred," said John. "Take all you want." The Coopers dominated the sport in

1959 and 1960, rarely won after that as first Brabham, then McLaren went off to build their own cars. Cooper ceased racing in 1968. John Cooper died on Christmas Eve, 2000

77: Ferraris being unloaded from the transporter, Grand Prix of Belgium, 1962.

78–79: Jack Brabham's Lotus arriving at the circuit, 1962 Belgian G. P. Brabham's own Brabham was not yet ready. As a one man private entry, he had no need of oversized transporters.

80: The paddock at Rouen, July 6, 1962. It is early morning before the last practice for the French G. P. Graham Hill is at extreme right of the photo facing the camera.

81: Rouen, same day. A Porsche with its cowling removed is nearly all tanks.

82: Oct. 1961. Bonnier about to start in the 1,000 Kilometers of Paris at Montlhery, France.

83: Tony Maggs before practice for 1962 British G. P.

84–85: Louis Chiron directing the start of practice. Monaco, 1962.

86: The chicane at Monaco, 1962. The blur is Graham Hill in a BRM. The cars have come out of the tunnel at about 120 mph and now must wiggle through this chicane onto the promenade bordering the harbor. The watching nurses are bored. Beside them a stretcher waits emptily.

87: Stavelot Corner in Belgium during practice, 1961. The lead car is an Emeryson driven by Lucien Bianchi. The trailing car is the Ferrari of Phil Hill.

88: Aintree, England, during practice for 1962 G. P., the Cooper pits. Left to right: Pat McLaren, Paula Cooper, Beverly Jane, Gail Maggs.

89: Burneville bend, Belgium, during practice, 1962. This corner is taken at about 130 mph, the cars drifting outwards toward the rail fence. The turn is about half a mile long, and Clark in a Lotus, still close to the inside, is about in the middle of it. This is the turn where Chris Bristow was killed in 1960, the rail fence decapitating him, and where Stirling Moss crashed that same year.

90: The start of Burneville bend, 1962.

91: Phil Hill, Ferrari, approaching the Casino at Monaco in early morning practice, 1959. The street goes left at the Casino for about 50 yards, then turns 90 degrees right passing the entire length of the Casino. This was the Friday practice held each year from dawn to about 9 a.m. to avoid closing off the street and the shops three straight days for practice.

92: Phil Hill, Belgium, 1961.

93, top: Lotus mechanics Jim Endruweit talking to Ted Woodley.

93, bottom: Innes Ireland. The other man is Louis Stanley, one of the backers of BRM.

94, left: Rodriguez and wife, Sarita, waiting for a car to be made ready, Monza, Sept. 15, 1962.

94, right: Aintree, July 20, 1962, Ferrari mechanic, Emer Vecchi and engineer, Mauro Forghieri.

95: A Ferrari being adjusted, Holland, 1962.

96–97: Dan Gurney, Porsche, at Rouen early in the morning. The circuit there is composed of public roads and so cannot always be closed during key hours to permit practice. Most practice sessions are between 7 and 10 a.m.

98–99: Clark in Lotus practicing for 1963 Monaco G. P.

100: Keith Greene in a Gilby attempting to qualify for the 1962 German G. P. The Nürburgring is full of harrowing dips such as this one, which is called Brunchen. The wheels come off the ground as the car goes over the dip. Then the short plunge downhill, and then uphill steeply to the right.

101: Practice for 1959 Monaco G. P. Phil Hill in the Ferrari leads Brooks into Tobacconist Corner. The Ferrari's have their long snouts truncated to minimize shunts and to get more air to the engines on this slow circuit. The car in the background has just come through the chicane onto the promenade.

102: The Lotuses of Innes Ireland and Masten Gregory entering the South Curve at Monza, 1962. It was in slowing for this curve that Trips crashed the year before. Trips went off the road to the left and into the crowd behind the chicken wire fence. The car then tumbled down onto the verge again and stopped at approximately the extreme left-hand edge of this photo. The reinforced chainlink fence in the foreground here went up in 1962 to prevent such accidents in the future, and spectators were not allowed in the area to the left at all. Unfortunately, the chainlink fence is too high and too thick. Probably it would shoot down any high flying race cars; but it also prevents fans from seeing the cars. Fans can see through it only about ten yards to either side of where they are standing. I stood on the roof of a soft drink shack to make this photo. The fans, right, cannot see the cars as they round this turn. Incidentally, Monza is positively the worst race circuit in Europe from the press, spectator, and also driver point of view. The regulations governing the movements of all are very strict, very limited, and, some say, very stupid. In addition, Monza is not worth going to because you can see neither over nor through that chainlink fence.

103: Oporto, Portugal, August 1960.

104: Gurney, Aintree, 1962. Before World War II race cars often had removable steering wheels so drivers could get in and out more easily. Then the practice dropped out of use until the 1962 Porsche. Gurney and Bonnier, the Porsche drivers, were both six footers and needed the extra room.

105: Jean Behra, Ferrari, 200 Miles of Aintree, April 1959. Behra qualified way back, but won the race the next day when all the faster cars broke down. It was the last race he ever won. He was killed in a sports car race in Berlin later that year.

106: Graham Hill qualified fourth for the British G. P. at Aintree in 1962. His gloom in this picture was well founded. He finished only fourth the next day.

107: The Lotus garage near Monte Carlo, the eve of the 1962 Monaco G. P.

109: Surtees, Monaco, May 1964.

110: Phil Hill and Trips had adjacent rooms at the Annette et Lubin Hotel in Spa, before the Belgian G. P. in 1961. On race morning they stood like this on the balcony killing time, waiting to go out to the track.

111: Graham Hill lunches with Ginther in the restaurant of the Bouwes Hotel, Zandvoort, on the morning of the 1962 Dutch Grand Prix, a race won by Hill. Ginther finished far back.

112: Lorenzo Bandini waiting nervously on the morning of the 1962 Monaco G. P.

113: Mairesse fighting off autograph hunters, Belgian Grand Prix day, 1962. Mairesse crashed this day too. Photos are in this book.

114: The paddock at Rouen before the 1962 French Grand Prix. Bonnier is seen at right.

115: If you want to buy a Stirling Moss steering wheel, they are on sale at Aintree before the race at roughly $21.

116: Brabham tuning the engine of the first of his Brabhams to race. German Grand Prix, 1962. Jann Tauranac, aged 6, daughter of Brabham's designer, holds her ears.

117: Ferrari engine, Nürburgring, 1962 German Grand Prix.

118–119: BRM, rear view, Nürburgring, 1962.

120: Denis Jenkinson is the best known of all

motoring journalists because he rode with Moss in the record-breaking 1955 Mille Miglia. He was the navigator, reciting detailed course directions throughout. A small man with a red beard, Jenks is also a former champion sidecar motorcycle racer. Nürburgring, 1962.

121, left: John Bolster, here working for the BBC.

121, right: Photographer, Monaco, 1962, name unknown.

122: Nürburgring, just before the start, 1962.

123: Trintignant, about to drive a Cooper, 1959, Lisbon.

124: Richie and Jackie Ginther, Rouen, July 1962. Their first son was born Oct. 6, 1962.

125: Phil Hill, before 1962 German G. P.

126, top: McLaren, 1962 German G. P.

126, bottom: Mairesse and friend, 1962 Monaco G. P.

127: Marianna Bonnier, Monaco, 1962.

128: Olivier and Marie-Claire Gendebien, Le Mans, 1960. Ironically, Marie-Claire died in a road accident a few years later. Gendebien himself died in 1998 at the age of 74.

128–129: Monaco 1960; the drivers receive last-minute instructions from the starter. Left to right: Ireland, Alan Stacey, Brooks, Moss (who won the race), Chris Bristow (in dark glasses), McLaren, Phil Hill, Ginther (crouching), Trips, Gurney (partially hidden), Bonnier, Roy Salvadori. Stacey and Bristow were killed a month later, and Trips in Sept. 1961.

130: Toto Roche about to start the French Grand Prix, July 8, 1962. Clark, foreground, and Surtees are the two heads which can be seen.

132: Gurney, Graham Hill, start of German G. P. won by Hill, Aug. 5, 1962.

133: Trips, German G. P., 1961. He finished second.

134–135: Phil Hill, German G. P., 1961. He finished third.

136, top: Intercontinental race, Silverstone, England, May 1961.

136, bottom: 1960 Portuguese G. P., Oporto.

138, top: Start of French G. P., Reims, 1960. Left to right: Lucien Bianchi, Maurice Trintignant, and Graham Hill. All three cars were wrecked. No drivers were hurt. The starter, Toto Roche, is too fat to move the starting flag up and down. He moves it sideways, which is one of the reasons this crash happened. Roche starts races with a great deal of drama, screaming, and arm waving. Most drivers detest him cordially, and one or two have written unkindly of him in their books. But he is the type of enthusiast without whom motor racing would perish. He is the driving force behind the French Grand Prix. He does, and causes to be done, a colossal amount of detail work. For this all he asks is to be allowed to start races. Usually he starts them much better than here.

138–39, bottom: Ireland stalled on the line, Aintree, 1962 British G. P.

140–141: Monaco, just after start, 1959. In a few yards the cars will turn 180 degrees back along the street paralleling this promenade. They race along this street to the inside corner of the harbor, then 90 degrees right up the hill under the BP Energol sign. This hill, much steeper than it looks, leads up to the Casino. From the Casino the street plunges back down to the railroad station, then onto the harbor front promenade again at the extreme right of this photo. The famous chicane onto the promenade would be some yards to the right of where this photo ends. A year or two after this photo was made the Monaco building boom began—now in 2005 it is still going on. All the villas and low buildings seen here were demolished, most of the medium-sized structures as well, even some of those that were already taller than anything else, and skyscrapers began to *rise that were higher than anything else on the Riviera, anything else in France. There must be fifty of them by now, perhaps more. Monaco no longer resembles this photo. These days it more closely resembles Hong Kong, or even Manhattan.*

142: 1962 Belgian G. P.

143: 1962 Dutch G. P.

144-145, top: 1959 Portuguese G. P., Lisbon.

144–145, bottom: 1960 Portuguese G. P., Oporto.

146: Colin Chapman, 35, the owner-designer of Lotus, at Aintree, 1962, British G. P. With his many innovative designs, including the first monocoque chassis and, later, the use of wings to hold cars tight to the road, Chapman is credited with having changed the face of motor racing. He died of a heart attack Dec. 16, 1982. He was 54.

147: Betty Hill, Monza, Italian G. P., 1962.

148: Monza, 1962 Italian G. P., the wide straight in front of the pits. In the background can be seen the speed banking which is sometimes used in conjunction with the road circuit for this race. The road circuit is flat. Shaped like a boomerang, it is 3.6 miles around, and is lapped at about 123 mph. In years when the banked oval is used in conjunction with the road circuit the lap distance is increased to 6.2 miles per lap and the speeds will average over 130.

149: 1962 Brussels G. P. This race does not count for the world championship, but is normally the first race of the European season and extremely interesting for this reason.

150–151, top: Brabham's Cooper leads Phil Hill's Ferrari in 1960 French G. P.

150–151, bottom: Phil Hill in a Ferrari, in second place, Clark's Lotus, in third, in 1961 Dutch G. P.

152: Ginther's BRM leads Salvadori's Lola and Taylor's Lotus on the back stretch at Aintree, 1962 British G. P.

153: Bandini just past Brunchen in a new, experimental Ferrari, Nürburgring, 1962.

154, top: Portuguese G.P. 1959, Moss, driving a Cooper, the Lisbon circuit providing splendid views of the Tagus River and the harbor.

155, bottom: Same race the following year but at Oporto. Considering the number of times and places where cars have sailed into grandstands, this setup looks unsafe. The crowds seem to have been allowed in much too close.

156: Behra's Ferrari leads Moss's Cooper up the steep hill to the Casino, 1959 Monaco G. P.

157: Spectators during 1962 Monaco G. P.

158, left: Pushing away Phil Hill's Ferrari, 1962 British G. P.

158, right: Usually drivers are philosophical about breakdowns. Often they know in advance, due to a structural weakness that there has been no time to fix, that they will break down. Others like Brabham are worried and depressed. This day, the 1962 German G. P., he had raced the first Grand Prix Brabham for the first time. The car not only failed, but was not particularly fast while it lasted. On this machine rides Brabham's future as a factory owner and builder, and he is deeply worried as he sits on the pit counter staring straight ahead. The car has failed for the day; for all he knows, it will fail forever. (In fact, in 1966 the car won Brabham his third world championship.)

159, top: Ireland rides piggyback on the car of Trintignant, 1961 Belgian G. P.

159, bottom: Hill signs official "retirement advice" for officials.

160, top: Phil Hill, Ferrari, during 1962 Dutch G. P.

160 bottom: Graham Hill, BRM, during same race. Graham won and Phil was third.

161: Ginther, Aintree, 1962.

162: 1962 Dutch G. P.

163: 1962 Dutch G. P.

164: Bonnier passing Mairesse who is stalled after a spin. (This photo and the next four are from the 1962 Brussels G. P.)

165: Trevor Taylor, half in rain gutter, tries to pass Mairesse, moments later.

166: Taylor shouting at Mairesse in same race.

168: Driver passing Taylor's wrecked Lotus is Joseph Siffert.

169: Taylor gets help in pushing his car off road.

170–171: Brooks' Ferrari passing triple collision on hill up to Casino in 1959 Monaco G. P. On second lap Trips lost control of his silver Porsche (No. 6), which spun and was bashed by the Lotus of Bruce Halford (No. 44) and the Ferrari of Cliff Allison (No. 52). Aside from facial cuts, no one was hurt.

172, top: 1962 Monaco G. P.

172, bottom: Trips in the 1960 Portuguese G. P.

173: 1962 British G. P.

174, top: Gurney, 1962 Dutch G. P.

174, bottom: Surtees, 1962 British G. P.

175, top: Ginther, 1962 Dutch G. P.

175, bottom: Moss, 1962 Brussels G. P.

176: 1962 Monaco G. P. The blur is Graham Hill's BRM, which led the race at this point but later broke down. Offshore is a launch bearing frogmen, in the event that a race car goes into the drink. This has happened only once, in 1955. Alberto Ascari, twice a world champion, was leading the race in a Lancia. He lost control in the chicane and plunged in. He came to the surface at once, as did much steam, but no race car. Frogmen fished him aboard, and he hid below decks from embarrassment. Ascari was killed while testing a car four days later, possibly because of fainting spells this plunge had caused and which Ascari did not realize he was subject to.

177: Baghetti's Ferrari (No. 50) and Bonnier's Porsche (No. 10) wheel-to-wheel during final laps of 1961 French G. P. This was Baghetti's first Grand Prix race, and he won it. Mairesse, right, who had broken down earlier, looks on. The cars were passing all these people at about 160 mph.

178: Mairesse in a Ferrari, 1962 Monaco G. P.

179: Dino Pignatti, Ferrari mechanic, same race. These signals were being flashed to Phil Hill who, with six laps to go, was second by 15 seconds and closing fast.

180: Clark in a Lotus in 1962 Monaco G. P.

181: 1962 Monaco G.P. John Cooper urges the race leader, Bruce McLaren, to go faster. With two laps to go, McLaren's Cooper led Hill's Ferrari by only five seconds.

182: Brabham leads Phil Hill during 1962 Monaco G. P. coming out of Tobacconists Corner.

183: Betty Brabham, during 1960 Portuguese G. P.

184: Phil Hill wins 1961 Belgian G. P. a few yards ahead of Trips. The third car in photo is a lap behind.

185: Brabham winning 1960 Dutch G. P.

186: McLaren, 1962 Monaco G. P. He has just won, just stopped, and people are running up to congratulate him.

188: Trips, 1961 Dutch G. P. The winner is standing up in his seat. The police are holding back professional photographers with official passes, but the little boys have gotten through.

189: Clark, 1962 British G. P.

190: Graham Hill, 1962 German G. P.

191: Moss with admirers, 1960 Monaco G. P. Princess Grace is bored stiff by the race, but must attend the start and finish each year. Prince Rainier loves the sport, used to race, and once crashed, though while using an assumed name. When the Grand Prix is underway each year, Grace and Rainier go high up in a nearby skyscraper; Rainier watches from a balcony while Grace reads.

192: Rouen, 1962 French Grand Prix. The race is over. Most cars will slow down while driving an extra lap, 4.1 miles more at the wheel. But here, two hundred yards past the finish line, Trintignant has jammed on the brakes and attempted to stop in front of his pits. Taylor came past the finish line at 160, intending to take an extra lap, but 200 yards ahead was Trintignant's car, nearly stopped, blocking the road. Taylor plowed into Trintignant. People screamed, dust rose, there was a tremendous noise. Photographers are already running toward the wreckage. Only one gendarme, and Colin Chapman (in white shirt) are worried about other cars which are still hurtling towards the finish line at 160. As this picture was made, both drivers are standing, staring at each other. Neither is hurt, but the two cars are write-offs.

194: The BRM of Graham Hill has spun, ramming the timer's box and spilling its occupants into the street. Hill, climbing from the wreck, murmured, "I'm terribly sorry." Two timers were hospitalized. Scene is Monaco, during 1960 G. P. Flag marshal attempts to slow down passing cars, here Brooks' Cooper, but this is no longer necessary.

195: In practice for the 1964 Dutch Grand Prix the BRM of Tony Maggs plunged through this chain link fence and down the embankment, coming to rest upside down with Maggs still in it. Some daylight showed under the cockpit. Maggs hung there. A Dutchman ran up, stuck his head up close and in his best high school English shouted in to Maggs: "What you want?" Several spectators lifted the car enough for Maggs to scramble out. He was unhurt.

196: Dutch G. P., 1962. Ireland's Lotus has shot off the road while braking at the end of the straight, possibly because a single wheel locked. The car plowed under the wire fence in the background and ended up against a dune.

197: Ireland, is shown here badly shaken. His shirt is torn and he is bleeding about the face.

199–203: Belgian G. P., 1962, late in the race. Mairesse's Ferrari, trailing by a foot or two, has brushed the Lotus of Taylor. Mairesse lies on the hillside above the wreck. Taylor is unscratched.

204: The burning Ferrari.

205–206: The Lotus. Its mechanics have raced over from the pits. But their driver is unhurt, and now there is certainly nothing they can do for the car. The mechanics are Cedric Selzer and Colin Riley.

207: The Trips crash occurred on the second lap of the 1961 Grand Prix of Italy. Trips collided with the Lotus of Clark as he attempted to move in front of Clark and set himself up for the turn shown on page 102. Television camera on the stand shown in that photograph shot everything, but the cars were moving so fast that every frame is blurred and it is impossible to know exactly what happened. Clark was later charged with homicide by imprudence, but was absolved.

208: Trips, after winning the Dutch G. P., 1961.

218: Graham Hill, with Betty trailing, after winning 1962 German G. P.

Index